Go M.A.D.

(Make A Difference)

Go M.A.D.
(Make A Difference)

SHOWING LOVE TO OTHERS THROUGH JESUS' LIFE

M. A. COOKSON

XULON PRESS

Xulon Press
2301 Lucien Way #415
Maitland, FL 32751
407.339.4217
www.xulonpress.com

Paperback ISBN-13: 978-1-66287-233-4
Ebook ISBN-13: 978-1-66287-234-1

Table of Contents

- ONE -

The World Today Needs Christ's Love

The world today is so full of doom and gloom. Everywhere you look, you see negativity and hate. It's on the news. It's on social media. It's in the songs that play on the radio. It is even in the ads you hear and see. This world desperately needs the light of Christ shining.

Nowadays, there are so many things that try to tell you what is right. How we should live and how we should treat one another. The world wants us to be okay with whatever a person is doing. The world focuses on us just being good people. Don't say or do anything that would offend them. I believe we should be nice, kind, and good to our fellow humans and treat them like the precious valuable people they are. This is what Christ did while he was on Earth. But, if we are believers in Christ, we should follow the example that God gave us in His Word and not the examples of the world.

The Bible shares many examples of how we should act and treat one another. I believe we need to look to the Bible for even more of Christ's examples. Looking at the Word for how we should treat one another is not a popular thing in society today. Society looks at the Bible as an old book that isn't relevant today, and views it as just an outdated history book. It is said to be a book that doesn't treat people equally. There are a lot of people who proclaim that they believe in God who would say the Bible is just a suggestion book or that only parts of it are relevant today. I think the Apostle John described the Bible best in John 1:1 (NIV), "In the beginning was the Word, and the Word was with God, and the Word was God. He was with God in the beginning." The Bible is called the Word of God, and the Word is God. So, if God is who He says He is, then how can His Word be outdated? How can His Word *not* be relevant today? How can only parts of His Word be truthful? God's Word is living today because it is relevant today. If we call ourselves Christians, then we should be following His Word.

God Himself loves us so much. He knew the only way that He would allow us in His presence was to give us His son who He loved very much. God sent us His son to be our bridge to Him and to be an example of how we should act. When I was in college, I took a web design class where we had to design a website using graphics. I was on fire for God, so I designed a website that showed that we needed Christ to get to God. It was a simple design that showed the Word 'Us' on one side and a big void of a hole and then the word 'God' on the other side. In that hole, I placed a graphic of a cross. It came down from the sky and landed perfectly between Us and God. Christ is the bridge between Us and God. The cross represents a bridge to God.

US  GOD

As believers in Christ, we should first and foremost look to the Bible, the living Word of God, on how we should live. I would like to invite you to go back to the basics of how children of God should act. Let's start with the basics of God's Word and Jesus who God sent to be the ultimate example for us, and then move onto God's commandments.

God wants a relationship with His creation. He wants His creation to love him like a child loves their Father. God already had angels that would sing His praise all day every day. God created the earth and all of the animals upon it and everything was good. God created man and woman in His image, and He said it was very good. God had the relationship that He wanted. A relationship where man wanted to spend time with Him because they were grateful to God. Like any good parent, God took care of His children. He provided them with a beautiful garden to enjoy. He provided them with clean water to refresh themselves. God provided them with food to eat. Man didn't have to work the ground for food. He sheltered them. Anything Adam and Eve needed God gave them. For a little while, Adam and Eve gave God what He desired, daily strolls through the garden with them. Adam and Eve had a perfect relationship with their Creator, Provider, and Father.

Although God had the perfect design, Man wanted something more. I still can't fathom how Adam thought there was anything more than what God had already given him. Adam and Eve were the rulers of the earth. They were given the charge of naming all the animals on the land and in the sea. They were in complete fellowship with their father. He was not a demanding father, either. He gave them one rule to follow. Sadly, this man could not follow that one rule, and from that moment on, we humans were on a downward spiral. Man and woman were removed from God's presence, and they had to learn to survive without their Father. Even after breaking His rule, God still loved His creation and took care of it. He gave man and woman knowledge to survive and the food and water they needed to stay alive.

Not only was He supplying them with the means to survive, but He was also orchestrating in the background a way to allow His people, His creation, back into His presence. At first, God would allow His people to be in His presence at certain times of the year only if they would show Him honor by bringing Him a gift, or an atonement, for the offenses that they made towards Him. Those atonements came in many different forms, and the most sacred form was a sacrificial lamb. God didn't want just any old lamb. He demanded a young lamb that was spotless and without blemish. In this, God was asking man to give Him their best. But that wasn't God's final plan to bring His people back into a relationship with Him. God demanded that perfection be given as a sacrificial lamb. The only way God could get that perfection was for part of Himself to come down to the earth to be that sacrificial lamb. So, that is what He did.

He came down and entered the world through a human woman and was named Jesus. Jesus in Hebrew means 'to deliver.' Even His name was a clue to who He was. Jesus came to this earth to be the final "end all" sacrifice. But that wasn't His only purpose on this Earth. God knew that we needed examples of how we are to live to bring joy to him. God needs us to know what makes Him happy and what makes Him sad. God knew that we needed examples of how to treat ourselves and how to treat others. From the beginning it has been Satan's goal to deceive, starting with Adam and Eve, even tempting Jesus himself. God's children, the Kingdom of Israel, were so full of themselves that they didn't know what love was. They thought they knew what was best for mankind. Jesus had to show us through His teaching and examples what real love looks like.

- TWO -

What is Love?

A Pharisee asked Jesus (God's son) "What is the greatest commandment?" This question wasn't asked because the people wanted to know His opinion. No, it was asked because the people wanted to trap Jesus. Little did the people know that they were talking to their Creator, and He knew what was in their hearts. Jesus answered them by saying "Love the Lord your God with all your Heart, with all your soul, and with all your mind. Second, love your neighbor as you love yourself" (Matt 22:37-39 NIV). He was telling us that three things are going on here. First, we are to love God. The Greek word that is used here for the word love is Agape, which is unconditional love. We are supposed to love God unconditionally with all our hearts, soul, and mind. Second, we are to love ourselves. Not in a selfish way, but in a way that glorifies him. We are created in God's image. We are His creation and have been made in His likeness. God wants us to be happy with how He molded us. We are all different but we have a common link and He is that link. It is said that beauty is in the eye of the beholder and this case, God is the beholder. We should find joy in the fact that He created us just the way we are. The third is dependent on the second one. I'll repeat that because this is very important. The third is dependent on the second. We can't love others unless we first love ourselves. We are supposed to love our neighbors. This is where the people back in Jesus' day failed. Their definition of a neighbor was not the same as Jesus' definition of neighbor. They were thinking that their neighbor was a person that was just like them. Someone who was a Hebrew that followed the commandments as they did. But, in this case, Jesus is telling us to love EVERYONE. He isn't telling me to specifically love my neighbor who lives across the street. Jesus wants us to love everyone. Those who look the same as us, and those who don't. Those who worship God our creator and those who don't believe in Him. Those who live down the block and those who live on the other side of the world. Anyone whom we have contact with is our neighbor, and they deserve God's love. We live in a very connected world now, and we can impact someone positively or negatively through what we do. Before we can love someone, we need to know what love is. We need to know the definition of love.

Love can mean many things in the English language. According to Webster's Dictionary, the definition of love is "A noun – strong affection for another arising out of kinship or personal ties. (2) affection based on admiration, benevolence, or common interests. (3) a warm attachment, enthusiasm, or devotion."

It can be a noun you say of your parents, "My mother's love for me is great" or "I have a love for the Pittsburgh Steelers, the best football team ever." We even say that we have a love for our car or our favorite pair of shoes. Love can also be defined as a verb. Webster's Dictionary's definition of love as a verb is "to hold dear (2) to feel a person's passion, devotion, or tenderness for (3) to like or desire actively and (4) to thrive in."

Love as a verb is an action. We show love by doing things for others. We ask in the question, do you love me? In this book, we will focus on love as an action rather than an emotion. God calls us to a command of love, which is an action. As one of the famous Christian bands from the '90s (DC Talk) said, "Luv is a verb."

God showed love to His creation; God demonstrated love by sending His son Jesus. During Jesus' time on earth, there were different words used to express different types of love. The most common words were Philia, which means brotherly love or a brotherly bond; Eros, which was a romantic love between men and women; Agape, which is unconditional love. This is the type of love that God showed us when He sent His Son to earth. This is the type of love God showed Jonah when He shaded him in Jonah 4:6. God showed this type of love throughout the Old Testament, and it is what the whole New Testament is about. When Jesus talked about the love of the father it was always the Agape type of love. He even told His disciples that His love for them was Agape love.

If Jesus Himself showed unconditional love to the people He met, then we as His followers are to do the same thing. There are many examples of Jesus showing love through action. One example is the Samaritan woman at the well. In the days of Jesus, the Jewish people did not associate with the people of Samaria because they grew up on the "wrong side of the tracks." Jews were taught throughout their lives that they were better than the Samaritans, and they were not to be seen with them. The Jewish people in Jesus' day were a lot like that group of kids in your high school that thought they were better than you. The Jewish people reminded the Samaritans every chance they could that Jews were better than Samaritans. But Jesus, in all His wisdom, decided to sit down by a well right when he knew a woman would be coming there. He started a conversation with her. I'm sure she was shocked by the fact that a Jewish man was speaking to her. Jesus asked her to fetch Him some water from the well. Jesus told her that if she knew who He was she would be asking Him for living water. He was telling a Samaritan woman, who was supposed to be a lowly human, that He was the Messiah, the Son of the living God. He showed her love by talking with her. She was a woman who had been married five times and was currently living with a man who was not her husband. Back in those days, that was not the type of woman Jewish men were supposed to be conversing with. But Jesus wasn't a typical Jewish man. He was and is the Son of God, and He loved all mankind.

Jesus not only showed unconditional love to people, but he also had compassion for people. When he would see a blind person reaching out for help, he had compassion for them. When His friend Lazarus died from an illness, Jesus wept and compassion overflowed out of him. He asked His dead friend to rise in John 11 and Jesus showed compassion on the woman with an issue of bleeding who believed that if she could just touch the hem of His coat that she would be saved in Luke 8:43-48. Not once in any of these examples did Jesus rebuke the person who was seeking His compassion. He freely gave it.

Jesus cared for all the Pharisees that tried to trick him. He cared for the Samaritan women at the well. He cared for blind people who were seeking help. He cared for the soldier who was sent to bring him before the high court. A soldier who was trying to arrest him got his ear cut off, and Jesus cared so much about him that he healed the ear. Jesus cares about us, also. He endured the pain of whippings to save us. He endured the humiliation of the cross because he cared for us. He cared for us so much that he decided to come down from Heaven, from His posh, comfy seat, to be a sacrifice for us.

A sign of Agape love is kindness. God showed kindness in many ways. In the days of Moses, God showed His people kindness by providing them with manna (unleavened bread) every morning for years. God showed His people kindness by sending Jesus to this earth. Jesus showed kindness throughout His time on Earth. He taught the people how to love God and how to live for God. He showed kindness by healing people. Kindness is a simple rainbow after rain. Kindness is a smile at a child. Kindness was shown by Jesus spending time with the little children. Kindness is caring for widows and parentless children. Kindness is one of the simplest ways that we can show love. Kindness is putting love into action.

The world's view of love

What is the world's view of love? When I am talking about the worldview, I mean a view that is not the same as God's. God created this world, but then Satan, a fallen angel (he thought he could be above God), corrupted this earth. When that happened, Satan began to roam the earth and influence people to turn away from God. Satan has been manipulating humans since the fall of man. Satan introduced the idea of disobeying God in Adam and Eve's heads. They disobeyed God, and that was what caused man to fall. Disobeying God is sinning against God, and sin is rampant on earth these days. Sin is something you don't read about in history books. To keep it simple, sin is just going against God's laws or word. After man fell from perfection, Satan was allowed to roam the earth, and roam he does. He will twist our thoughts to make us believe him and to believe the things that contradict God's words and laws. Satan will use many different platforms to do his dirty work. He will use marketing, social media, television, radio, music, and movies. Satan has used all of these things to twist our view of what love is. Let's look at Satan's twisted views of love. They are selfishness, lust, greed, self-satisfaction, and pride.

Selfishness

God intended for love to be something that lifts another, but the world has twisted it to make people think that love should be all about themselves. We were created with a desire in us to care about others and to be relational beings. In the beginning, God created Adam to care for and nurture the Earth and its creatures and to have fellowship with God. But once sin entered our lives, everything changed. The world will tell us that we need to worry about ourselves before anyone else. It has even found a way to twist selfishness to sound less harmful. Nowadays we hear phrases such as "take time for yourself," "it's self-care," or "I need me time." There is nothing wrong with taking care of ourselves, but when we decide that we are more important than the other people in our inner circle, that is selfishness. Webster's Dictionary definition of the word selfish is "concerned excessively or exclusively with oneself: seeking or concentrating on one's own advantage, pleasure, or well-being without regard for others." I am talking about that type of behavior. While driving down the interstate a few weeks back, I noticed a billboard. The ad was about traveling, and it said, "You deserve to get away from the worries of your life." A person was sitting on a plane while in the corner you saw their family at home. This is just one example of the type of advertising we see daily that urges us to be selfish. Movies are normally filled with the main character that cares more about themselves than the people around them. For example, take the movie National Lampoon's Vacation. The main character, Clark, is so self-focused on his desires for the perfect vacation, that he doesn't think about his family's wants. We are bombarded with images on social media that promote self-care.

Lust

The world's view of sex, pleasure, and intimacy is not the same as God's. Since God created man and woman, he was the one who created sex. God created pleasure and intimacy, but we are only supposed to have that pleasure after we are in a God-ordained marriage. Satan uses lust to get people away from God's true purpose for sex. While driving in my vehicle recently, I flipped the radio over to a '90s station. As soon as I flipped to the channel, a song about sex came on. Lust is on the radio, in the movies, and on TV. It is crazy to see how common sexual situations have become on prime-time

TV over the last ten years. My wife and I were talking around Easter about how much TV has changed in the last decade. Ten years ago, you could still see the Easter story on Easter Sunday on one of the big TV networks. Now on Easter, you don't see the story of the resurrection, but you see unmarried people hooking up. That is not the design that God has for a relationship between a man and a woman. His design from the beginning of Genesis was one man and one woman. Once that man and woman came together, they were one.

Greed

Greed is the love of things. We put more effort into loving our money than loving God. We put more effort into loving our cars than loving God. We put more effort into loving our houses, jobs, and relationships than we do loving God. I could go on and on about all the things the world tells us we need to be the objects of our affection. We are constantly bombarded with ads telling us what we need. You can't go on social media without seeing something the world is pushing. We are constantly being told that the more stuff we have, the better off we will be. I am a car guy and there are times that I have to check myself to see where my head and heart are. In the summer when it's beautiful, I like to hand wash my car, but if I start doing that every day or every other day, then I am putting too much of my effort into taking care of that car.

There is nothing wrong with enjoying the blessings that God has given us, but when we care more about the blessing than the blesser, then our hearts have been deceived. We can have nice things while living on earth as long as those things don't become our gods. If I don't check myself, I can make my car a god to me because I am putting that object above other things. I can do the same thing with my family. We are supposed to love and cherish our family, but we aren't supposed to put our family above God. The world, on the other hand, wants us to spend our time and efforts on the things of this earth. It wants us to have those desires of that nice sports car. It wants us to spend hours thinking about new toys. If the world can get our focus on objects, then we can't focus on the Creator. When we put our focus on the things of this world, then Satan can slip more and more of himself into our world. And sooner or later, we will look up and see that our focus is on things of this earth and not on our Creator. This is one of the reasons that God gave the commandment "You shall not make for yourself an image in the form of anything in heaven above or on the earth beneath or in the waters below. You shall not bow down to them or worship them; for I, the Lord your God, am a jealous God" (Gen. 20: 4-5 NIV). God knows that he has competition when it comes to what/whom we love.

Self-satisfaction

Webster's Dictionary defines self-satisfaction as "a feeling of being very pleased or satisfied with yourself and what you have done." This is something that is very commonplace in society today. We have the belief that we have earned the right to care about ourselves more than anyone else, and we take pride when we do something better than others do. We think that we only have this one life to live, so we had better take care of ourselves. If I have had a bad day at work, then I deserve to go out for a drink with the guys after work instead of going home and spending the evening with my wife or kids. I just got a huge promotion at work, so I deserve a new toy. Hanging out with your friends is not a bad thing and buying yourself a gift is not a bad thing. It becomes destructive, however, when you are putting yourself over the needs of those you love.

Pride

Pride is the mindset that I am better than others, so I matter more than others. We see this mentality throughout American society. We Americans pride ourselves on being the best we can be. It is the American Dream to be successful. Some people take the American Dream even further. They will push other people down just to get further ahead in life, and if called out, they get offended. Their pride has gotten the best of them.

We need to stop being selfish if we want to have the love of God running through our hearts. Stop looking at yourself and start looking at others. Here are a few questions I want to ask about God and His actions toward us. Was God being selfish when he sent His son to be born on this earth? Was God being selfish when he commissioned Jesus to have compassion for the sick? Was God being selfish when he allowed Joseph to go through pain so that Israel wouldn't be lost to a famine in Genesis 37:50? Was God being selfish when he sent Moses to Egypt to bring the people of Israel out of slavery and oppression in Exodus 3:13? Was God being selfish when he fed the whining Israelites with manna in Exodus 16?

All these examples from the Old Testament show God being selfless while the people of Israel were being selfish. Even though

God's people whined and complained about being out in the wilderness, God still showed His love. He fed them every day, and when the people complained about only having bread to eat, he then provided the people with birds to eat. This should be the example of love that we are looking at and not how the hottest celebrity is acting or how the government is treating people. The difference between worldly love which is distorted and God's perfect love is that God by his very nature is love in itself. As Christians, we need to look at God's Word to know how to love. Next, we will look at Jesus' view of love by looking at loving God with our hearts, soul, and mind. We will also look at loving ourselves (not in a selfish way) and loving our neighbors.

Jesus' view of love

One of the most famous passages in the Bible is John 3:16. "For God so loved the world that he gave His one and only son, that whoever believes in him shall not perish but have eternal life" (NIV). This is God's view of love. It is a type of love that is selfless. God loved us so much that he gave up part of himself for us. He gave part of himself up so we could spend our lives with him. God's vision of love is His desire for us to be with Him. This desire is why Jesus had to come to the Earth and why He had to die on the cross. God set the standard for Israel on how to atone for their wrongdoings against him. God demanded a pure lamb as a sacrifice. Why did he demand a pure lamb? Because the pure lamb is the best lamb of the flock that a person could give. God wants us to give him our best. He wants us to give him praise for creating us. God wanted the sacrifice to be a sacrifice from His people. He wanted them to feel the effect of what it was like to give away their best. What they got in return was an atonement for their sins.

Atonement is just another way of saying forgiveness for their sins. In the old covenant, atonement only lasted for some time. The people of Israel had to continually give sacrifices to God to atone for their continuing sins. But God had a better plan for that atonement. One great sacrifice would make atonement for His people, and all people, for good. It wasn't even a sacrifice they had to give to God. It was a sacrifice God gave to His people to atone for our sins. Jesus was that sacrifice. Jesus' blood had to be spilled for us more than the lamb of the Israelites in Moses' time. Jesus' blood atones anyone who will accept His sacrifice. Jesus' view of love is devotion to His father. Throughout the gospels, you will see Jesus saying that he is doing His father's will. He is doing the work of His father.

Jesus is the ultimate example of selfless love. He gave His own life for all of mankind. Selflessness is the opposite of the world's view of love. This type of love is about putting the needs of others before yourself. Jesus talked a lot about how we need to be servants to others. Another view of Jesus' love for us is His charge for us to take care of others. Jesus told His disciples that they were to take care of the widows and orphans. He said that if we are His followers, then we will take care of those that can't take care of themselves.

Another view of Jesus' love is that he has asked us to be His hands and feet to others. He asks us to always be willing to help others out. Not just your biological family or close friends but anyone. We should be willing to help out the elderly couple that we see at church. We should be willing to help the single mother we see at the store. We should be willing to help the drunk man we see stumbling out in front of a bar. We should be willing to help out the troubled woman who thinks that the only thing she has of value is her body. We are called to help every person who requires help. In Jesus' eyes, there are no stereotypes of people. There are no colors, there are no social classes of people. Every person is as precious as the next person in Jesus' eyes.

The last view of Jesus is giving to others. A very famous story in the Gospel of Jesus is about the boy who gave his fish and bread to Jesus in Matthew 14:15-21. When we talk or think about that story, we normally think about the miracle that Jesus performed by turning the two loaves of bread and five fish into enough to feed 5,000 men, women, and children. But I think we should take note of the fact that the boy gave what he had to help Jesus. I do not doubt that the boy was blessed by Jesus for his act of kindness. Normally, when Christians talk about giving, it is usually giving to the church, but that is not what I'm talking about. I am saying that we should be willing to give to people who are in need. We might see a lady at the store who is checking out and realize that she doesn't have enough money to pay for everything. Jesus might lay it on your heart to give her the rest of the money. You might see a friend from high school who has posted on social media that they need a ride to a doctor's appointment. You feel the Holy Spirit moving inside you so you answer that by saying you can give them a ride. Giving doesn't always have to involve money. It can be money, time, prayers, or food. We are to give of ourselves to others.

- THREE -

Why Love?

Why do we love? From the moment we were born, we were made to love. It might even be ingrained in us when we are being formed within our mother's womb. From the moment we are created, we are shown love. Our mothers care for us while we are inside their bodies. I am not a mother, but my wife is. I can remember when she was pregnant with our first child and she found out that she was pregnant, she did everything she could to take care of the child right away. She showed the baby love by eating well, taking vitamins, and exercising. Love is shown to us from the first day that we are known to our parents. Just like your earthly parents have loved you since you were created, your Heavenly Father has loved you too. Jeremiah 1:5 (NIV) reminds us "Before I formed you in the womb, I knew you, before you were born, I set you apart." God created you and, in that creation, he put His love in you.

"We love because He first loved us" (1 John 4:19 [NIV]). That is why we love. God first loved us, so he put that desire for love in us. We were created with love, it's in our spiritual DNA. We were created with the desire to give love to others and the desire to receive love from others. Love is an inward and outward display. Another part of our spiritual DNA is caring for others. Caring is an outward display of kindness and concern for others. Outward displays of love are in our DNA, demonstrated by caring for others. Respect is just another way to show that we care for others. Respect is an admiration for others. I show respect by opening the door of a restaurant for a pregnant woman or an elderly woman. It is helping those that need it and those who can't do something on their own. We all show love in different ways, and those ways are determined by how we have been shown love. Everyone will have different examples of what they have seen love look like.

One example of love is the love that our parents showed us. For many, it's the first example of what love is. Whether good or bad, the way they treated us was molding the way we saw love. My parents set a pretty good example of what love looked like. I never heard my parents call each other names. I never saw my parents use derogatory words toward each other. I saw my dad being affectionate towards my mom, probably more than I wanted to as a kid. But that was an amazing example for me of how I should treat my wife. My parents showed my sisters and me love by always taking care of each other and us. They didn't give us every material thing we wanted, but they gave us shelter, food, and affection. One of the best ways that they showed us love was by introducing us to Christ Jesus.

The second example of love is how the world shows us love. We discussed in the first chapter how the world views love. The world shows us its view of love through magazines, television, music, and social media. Magazines like Seventeen, Vogue, Self, etc. all have columns that will give us advice on relationships. The advice is usually focused on sexual satisfaction for the reader. Television (as our pastor always says) tells its vision to you. Television likes to tell its version of love to those watching. Back in the '50s, television showed families as a husband and wife married with kids who would show respect to each other. In "Leave it to Beaver," Mr. Cleaver always showed love to his wife through kind words and respectful adoration. Mrs. Cleaver always showed her love by respecting her husband.

Fast forward to shows in the 2000s. We now have shows where the focus is on families who are either single-parent families, blended families, or dysfunctional families. Unfortunately, these shows are just showing the reality of the world we live in. Many families are single-parent families. Many families are blended because the parents are divorced or in their second marriage. Many families are dysfunctional because that is the only thing they know. The problem is that the shows on TV are glorifying the dysfunction of the family and love for one another in negative ways. You have husbands that are out bowling with their buddies and trash-talking their wives. You have wives that are going to the park with other moms and are talking about how worthless their husbands are. Why glorify this? Because it's dramatic, and that is what people want to see. What you don't see much of on television are husbands praising their wives or wives that show their husbands respect when they are out with their girlfriends. The worst example that television gives us is daytime shows (soap operas). Those shows, as the Christian singer Carman said in his song, "Now we survive on the immoral lives of the young and the restless ..." As a kid during the summer, I watched a few soap opera episodes. How unfortunate that these shows are set as an example of love and respect. Network Television glamorizes immoral love as the gold standard of what love looks like. Unfortunately, that is what young kids will see as normal and right.

Music is another example of how the world depicts love. If you listen to any contemporary music, you are bombarded with a substandard example of love. Pop music is about hooking up with one another. If you listen to popular radio stations, you will hear about how the singer wants their lover to touch them. Or how they love the shape of their conquest's body. My wife and I were on vacation in Miami, and we decided to go to dinner at a Cuban restaurant that had a TV playing music videos. When we got there, the music they were playing was in Spanish and seemed tame. But the longer we were there, the more the music was sexualized. My wife and I talked about how this is one of the reasons the younger generation is the way they are. If you listen to modern non-Christian hip hop, you will hear all about illicit sexual rendezvous, drugs, or murder. On the same vacation as the Cuban dinner, my wife and I would walk on the beach during the day, and we would hear about ten different speakers playing music. Most of it was hip-hop, filled with disrespect, hyper-sexualization, and violence. It was disheartening to see the way the young people were singing to the music and how they were dancing to the music. No genre is immune, even country music glamorizes the same themes. Sure, when I think about country music, I don't normally think about love songs. But there is quite a few out there. One in particular talks about trying to get over a breakup, and the way they do that is by falling into a bottle of whiskey and the arms of a stranger.

Social media is relatively new, but in our society, I believe it's one of the most damaging tools Satan uses to relay his messages. There are many different platforms out there that I could talk about, but I will talk about just a select few. One is a photo-sharing app. It was created so people could share the pictures that they have on their phones with other people. It has now turned into an app that promotes selfishness and perfection. I know that is not the purpose, and it's more the people on the app doing these things, but it encourages narcissism. While on vacation, my wife and I were sitting on the beach and were saddened by the number of people that had their phones out. They were taking pictures that were in inappropriate poses. They were trying to show off what they thought was their best asset. It seemed like everyone younger than us was doing this. They do it to get likes from other people. Another app uses 120 characters to grab the reader's attention. You can also post pictures and videos. Another app is where you can post stories about your life. Where you share your feelings, thoughts, pictures, and/or videos just to get likes and a thumbs-up. These social apps are all about getting approval from other people. Most of the time, it's people you don't even know. But if you can get enough views or likes then that means that you are loved by people. Honestly, isn't that what we all want? We all want to be loved and accepted by others.

The tools that the world uses to push an agenda or vision out are not bad inherently. It's the way that Satan has used them that makes them harmful to people. You wouldn't think that you would see the words love and hate being used in the same sentence. But that is exactly what Satan's view of love is to us. It is very harmful. Real love is not sex. Real love is not hooking up. Real love is not 100K views on a photo you posted. Real love is not a message that goes viral. Real love was created by God for His people to show their appreciation to him.

How then should we love? Which example should we follow? It is so easy to follow the examples the world shows us, as its influence is everywhere. It is no surprise that so many people throw the word love around so casually. It's not a surprise that the age that young people get married keeps going up. It's not a surprise that people don't follow the traditional ways of dating. Today people are so afraid of commitment that they will just go from one person to the next. So many people have a fear of true commitment, perhaps because of the relationships they saw growing up. Maybe their parents' relationship was a bad example. Maybe it was their aunts and uncles. Maybe it was the relationship between their parent's friends. We are all affected by our environment.

If you were raised by a family that showed you Christ's love, then you're blessed. Christ's love should be shown through all relationships. My prayer for all those reading this is that if you weren't raised in a household that demonstrated or cultivated Christ's love, you would take the steps to change the path of your family. We don't have to follow the examples the world has given us. We don't have to follow the examples that our parents showed us. I was raised in a Christian household. I was in church from the time I was a baby. But my parents weren't perfect. They didn't always show Christ's love to us. When I grew up and started my family, I pledged to myself that I would take all the good that I was taught by my parents and that I wouldn't bring non-Christ-like things into my family. I will admit that it can be hard at times, but it is possible. I purposefully try to show love every day. There are days that I am successful, and there are days when I crash and burn. I can remember a day when my kids were having a hard time listening and something got broken. I didn't show the love of Christ as I raised my voice. I sent my kids to their room so I wouldn't yell and escalate the situation. I started cleaning the house to calm myself down. I walked by my oldest daughter's room, and I saw her sitting on her bed praying. My heart broke. I had caused so much pain to my kids because I let my anger out. My daughter was in her room praying to God that I would not get mad anymore. How is it that a 7-year-old knew how to show more love at that moment than a 40-year-old man? I immediately went to God and asked for forgiveness. After that, I went to each child and asked them for forgiveness.

So, where do we start? All we need to do is look to God's Word to know how to love. Starting in the Old Testament and throughout the New Testament, God consistently shows His love. We have an instruction manual that is readily available to us that shows us how to love. We have a Heavenly Father who is available for us to cry out to. We have the Holy Spirit who wants to live inside of us and who will help us when we ask. God the Father, God the Son, and God the Holy Spirit are all gentlemen. They will never force themselves into your life. They will wait patiently for you to invite them in.

FOUR

Why is Jesus Christ Our Example of Love?

In the beginning was the Word, the Word was with God, the Word was God. He was with God in the beginning, through him all things were made; without him nothing was made that has been made. In him was life, and that life was the light of all mankind. The light shines in the darkness, and the darkness has not overcome it. John 1:1-5 (NIV)

There are two views to everything in this life. One view is the view of the world and the other view is the true view that God gave us. I grew up as a child of the '80s and '90s. When I was in high school science, they taught the two views of how this world was created. The big bang theory versus the Creation view from the Bible. The big bang theory states (in layman's terms) that there was an explosion and then matter happened. It states we come from a micro-organism evolving into a human being and that the process took millions of years. The big bang theory is the world's view of how the earth was created and how humans came into existence.

The Bible gives us a different view of how we came to be. God himself created us. God spoke and poof, the earth was here. I am a student of science, so I love to learn about different theories. The thought that we came from organisms like tadpoles and evolved into very smart beings is odd to me. I like that we have brains that allow us to come up with theories about things. But in the last twenty-five years or so, the science community has tried to make the Big Bang the core theory when it comes to how the earth came about. The world is pushing something that hasn't been proven as fact. The world is trying to cover up the real creation story. Why cover up the truth that a higher being created the world? Because Satan doesn't want us to worship God. He wants the praise and worship God deserves. He doesn't want the world to believe that God is real because if we believe God is real, then we will believe that Jesus is who he says he is. And if Jesus is who he says he is, then Satan must admit that he has been defeated. Satan cannot stand that he has lost. It all comes back to Jesus being real. *In the beginning, was the Word. In other words, in the beginning, Jesus was around, and Jesus was with God and Jesus is part of God.* I have always liked the verse John 1:1.

Ever since God created man, He has always planned to show His love. He first showed His love by creating us to be independent. We weren't created to be like a robot. We weren't programmed and hardwired to only do a specific task. God gave us free will to choose. Sadly, the first humans on the earth decided to look outside of God's love. They had been in a face-to-face fellowship with their creator. I can only imagine what it was like for Adam and Eve to take walks with God. I would guess it would be the same feeling we had as kids when our parents would take us on walks or when our parents removed all distractions and spent time with us. Adam and Eve decided to listen to a voice that told them a lie. The lie was that if they ate from the tree God told them not to eat from, they would be equal to God. Satan was using desire and pride to lure them into his plan. Once they went against God's desire for them, they knew they had disobeyed him. Their eyes were opened because of their sin, and I am sure they felt shame because of their decision.

But even in their disobedience, God still loved them. He will always love us. He came up with a way for His creation to continue to fellowship with him. He can only be in the presence of righteous beings. But because of the disobedience of man, we are not righteous. So, how can we become righteous? What is required by God to become righteous? There had to be a sacrifice given to God that would cover our sins. This is where Jesus said he would be willing to give Himself as that sacrifice. Jesus wanted to show His love for His people, so He decided he would be the sacrifice. Jesus was righteous. He became our sacrifice, so we could become righteous through Him.

Before Jesus came, God found a man, Abraham, that was honoring him, and through that man, God created a great nation (Israel). And even when that nation would turn its back on God, He still would show His love by forgiving them when they repented and turned from their sins. The nation of Israel became slaves in Egypt. God sent a descendant of Abraham named Moses to the Pharaoh of Egypt to set the people of Israel free. Through a series of conversations with the Pharaoh and then a series of plagues against the

Egyptians. God's people were freed of their slavery and fled Egypt. After fleeing Egypt, the Pharaoh changed his mind and sent his soldiers after God's people. God saved his people by parting the waters of the Nile River and then closing the waters over the soldiers from Egypt. God then led his people through the desert to a land that he had for them. When the nation of Israel complained about being led to the desert and not having food, God showed love. He gave them manna and birds to eat. God provided for them. When the people of Israel complained about not having a king like the other nations, God listened to them. God gave them kings. Not all of the kings were good to His people, but that was not His design. God protected His people when they were honoring him. God provided for them when they were honoring Him. God gave them knowledge about the coming messiah who would free His people. That messiah he told them about was Jesus. From the time of Abraham to the death of Jesus, God was providing for His people and showing them love.

Jesus is fully God and a full man. Jesus was born of the flesh, and because of that, we have a great example of how to live in the flesh. Because Jesus was still fully God, he knew all of the tricks of Satan and knew what humans needed. God knew that we not only needed a way to become righteous, but we needed an example of how to live. An example of how we should love. Throughout Jesus' time on earth, He didn't just talk about how we should act, He walked it out for us. On numerous occasions, Jesus was so moved by the hurting people around him that He would ask if they wanted to be healed, and if so, He would heal them.

Jesus, being fully God, had the right to judge people while He was walking on earth, but He chose not to. An example that comes to mind is the woman who was caught in the act of adultery in John 8:1-11. The religious leaders of the day brought a woman who they caught in adultery to Jesus to see if they could trap Him and accuse Him of false teaching. They asked Jesus what should be done to this woman. The law of the day was that any woman caught in adultery should be stoned. Jesus knew why they brought the woman, and He knew that they were trying to trap Him. He decided to squat down to the ground and write in the dirt. The Bible doesn't tell us what he was writing. I like to believe that he was writing about some of the sins that the religious leaders had committed. His next statement is what makes me believe this. When they kept badgering him, he told them that whoever is without sin should throw the first stone. One by one, from the oldest to the youngest left. The oldest with their maturity recognized they were in no position to cast that first stone. All the while, Jesus bent back down and wrote in the dirt. Once all the leaders had left, Jesus looked up to the woman and asked her where all of her accusers were. Was there anyone to condemn her? She replied to him that no one was there. He said that he did not condemn her either. This is Jesus, who was sinless. Of all the people there that day, he was the one who was without sin, yet he didn't condemn her. He didn't judge her. He showed her love by not judging her. He just lovingly asked her to go and sin no more.

Jesus outlined what love should look like in many parables. A parable is an earthly story with a heavenly meaning to it. There is a story in Luke 10:25-37 about a good Samaritan that I am going to paraphrase the story a little. Once again, the religious leaders were trying to test Jesus. They asked him what they must do to inherit eternal life. Jesus replied with a question: What is in the law and how do you read it? The leader replied, Love the Lord your God with all your heart and with all your soul and with all of your strength and with all of your mind and to love your neighbor as yourself. Jesus told them that they had answered correctly and that if they did that then they would live (meaning they would live with God for eternity). So, the leader went on and asked Jesus, Who is my neighbor? Jesus told the leader and the rest of the people around him a story. A Jewish man was going from Jerusalem to Jericho and on the way, he was attacked by a couple of big bad men. They took his clothes and his possessions. Then, they proceeded to beat him and left him in a world of hurt. A few minutes later, a Jewish priest came strolling down the same road, and when he saw the half-clothed and beaten man on the side of the road, he passed by on the other side of the road. A few minutes after that, a Levite (a Jewish man who is in the service of God) came down the same road and did the same thing as the priest. He also passed the half-clothed and beaten man on the other side of the road. A few minutes later, a Samaritan came down the same road. He saw the half-clothed and beaten Jewish man and compassion rose inside of him. He stopped next to the man, took some supplies he had, and bandaged and mended the man the best he could. He then helped the man up and put him on his ride. He took the man to an inn and took care of him there. The Samaritan had to leave the next day, but before he did, he gave the innkeeper money and asked him to look after the hurt man. He told the innkeeper that he would give him more money when he returned if the innkeeper earned it. After the story was over, Jesus asked the leaders which of those three men was the Jewish man's neighbor. Jesus told them to go and do likewise.

This story has been one of my favorites for many reasons. First, it shows that anyone and everyone is considered our neighbor. In those days, a Jew would not interact with a Samaritan. The Jews thought of the Samaritans as if they were inferior to the Jews. After Israel was captured by the Assyrians around 732 B.C., the Israelites that were captured started to intermarry with the Assyrians. The area would eventually become Samaria, and the Israelites that lived there were a mix between Jews and Assyrians. The full-blooded Jewish people didn't think too highly of the Samaritans. For a "half-breed" to be the hero of the story was kind of a wake-up call to the Jews. Jesus was saying that yes, we should love those who are ministers from God. Yes, we should love those who are from our own families. But we should also love those that are not exactly like us. We are supposed to love those people who might be a little rough around the edges. We are supposed to love the people who are getting drunk in the bar. Where someone is from doesn't matter to God. What someone looks like doesn't matter to God. Guess what? You and I once looked like those people. We were in the same position they are in. We were filled with our issues. But someone who wasn't like us had compassion and cared for us. They treated us like we were their neighbor. There are too many people in the world today that need to hear this. Where we come from or what we look like does not matter. When God looks at us, we all look the same.

He sees us through Jesus' blood. When we see sin, we think of some sins as being worse than others. We think of sin kind of like a bar graph. Lying is a little sin, Adultery is a big sin, etc... But from God's view in Heaven, he is looking down and he just sees sin horizontally. To God, it looks like a straight line.

The second thing God reveals in the parable is the heart of the characters. There are six or seven different characters in this parable. There are at least three Jews, all from the same country. There are one or possibly two Samaritans, the man who helped the victim, and the innkeeper could have been a Samaritan too. And then you have the robber(s) with unknown nationalities. We don't know much about the heart of the Jewish man who's the victim or the heart of the innkeeper. I'll focus on the Jewish men who did not stop to help, the good Samaritan and the robber(s).

First, let's look at the heart of the two Jewish men who refused to stop to help. They were important men by their titles, but their titles were just that. In their hearts, they weren't nice men. Why didn't they help the victim? I'm not sure if it was the fact that the hurt man was bloody and half-naked. Maybe they didn't want to ruin their clothes with another man's blood. Maybe they thought they were too busy and didn't have time for someone else. Or maybe it was the pride in their heart. The voice that says, "I'm too important to deal with a common person." Maybe it was something in their head that was saying that it was the man's sins, the man's fault that got him bloody and in the ditch. Maybe they thought he deserved it. You pick whichever one of those excuses you want (because that is what they all are, excuses). Ultimately the reason they didn't help was that their hearts were hardened. I will confess that there have been times when I have been the priest or the Levite in the story when I see someone in need. It's not that I was a bad person at that time; it was more that my heart wasn't focused on God and His love. I was too focused on myself and my desires.

Next, let's look at the heart of the good Samaritan. This was a man who was from a land that the victim didn't like. But his heart was not focused on the hate of the other group. His heart was focused on the compassion he had. His focus was on caring for a hurt person. The Samaritan didn't see a Jewish person. Instead, he saw a person in need. Back in those days, people didn't keep a first aid kit strapped to their donkeys. I'm sure the bandages that he used on the hurt man were from the clothes on his own back. He wasn't concerned about ruining his clothes. His heart was focused on love. We see a person who has their heart in the right place and helps. That is what Jesus is saying. We need to be the person who has our heart in the right place. We are to love one another with the love God has given us.

Finally, let's look at the robber(s). I believe the robbers represent the world or Satan. I know this might sound strange, but let's just go with it. The robbers took what wasn't theirs, beat the person up, and left him to die. John 10:10 (NIV) describes Satan just like that when it states, "The thief comes only to steal and kill and destroy." That resembles the world we live in today. The world we live in is not always kind to people. It is not kind to God's people. The world, just like the robbers, is out for itself. You can define the world how you want. There are people in the world that only care about themselves.

Some lifestyles are all about being number one. So, when I read this story, I see Satan as the robber. We also see the normally good-hearted people that are too busy to help and just pass by.

Another example Jesus gave us about demonstrating love is more of an example of how God loves us as found in Luke 15. This parable talks about the lost son or as some call it, the Prodigal son, and I will paraphrase it once again. The story tells of a father who has two sons. Let's call them Henry and Billy. The younger son, Billy, knew that his dad was a well-to-do businessman. Billy came to his dad and asked for his inheritance early so he could leave the family and go out on his own. His father, though saddened, agreed to the request.

Billy left his family and went to the big city and wasted all of the money he was given. He spent it on food, drink, expensive clothes, and women. He eventually ran out of money, and on top of that, there was a famine in their country. Billy got a job with a local farmer to do labor and work with the livestock. Billy was hungry and the only thing he could get his hands on to eat was the food given to the animals by the local farmer that hired him.

As the days in poverty went on and on, he realized that his father's servants had plenty to eat. Surely, his father would have compassion and let him come home and work for him so he could have a roof over his head and food to eat. Billy eventually decided that he was going to head back to his hometown and go to his father. On his trip home, he rehearsed what he would say to his father in his head. The script played over and over. He would tell his father that he made a mistake and that all he wanted was to come back and work for him.

One night, the father was outside of his house looking over his land when he saw his younger son coming towards the house. The father was so full of joy that he picked up his outer coat and ran to meet his son (verse 20). When Billy met his father, his father hugged and kissed him, but Billy stopped him.

Billy said to his father, "Father, I have sinned against you and heaven, and I am no longer worthy to be called your son."

His Father interrupted him, calling some of his servants over. He told them to go fire up the grill, put on some of their best steaks, grab his clothes, and put them on Billy. They were to grab some of his best jewelry and put it on his son as well. Call up my closest friends, and let's have a party. For my son who was lost has been found!

This story shows how much God loves us. The Father represented God, and Billy represents us, who are all sinners. God will love us no matter what we do. He loved us before we even knew who he was. If we get selfish and rebel, God still loves us. He rejoices when we come back to him and repent. Henry, the older brother, can represent us too, as Christians. His story is that he did everything that his father asked of him. He never went against his father's rules or requests. When Billy ran off, Henry was upset and had a few not-so-nice choice words for his brother. He might have even secretly been happy that his brother ran away as he would be recognized as the good brother. When Billy came back home and repented to his father, Henry was upset when he saw the party that the father threw for Billy. Henry would not and could not (because of his selfishness and pride) go to that party. The father came out to him and told him that he should be happy that his brother who was dead and lost, had come back. Henry represents Christians that have a holier-than-thou complex. The ones who think that they are better than others because of all the work that they do for God. The ones who look down on others because they are not the same. The ones who can't see past the sin. Even though the father had every right to throw the younger son a party and the older son had no right to throw a fit, the father came to the son to show him that he was loved too. God, our father loves us even when we aren't being very loving to others. He will come to us and show us love when we are being selfish and prideful. Both sons were sinners, just in different ways. God showed His love to both sons.

Another parable in Luke 15:4-6 that depicts God's love is about a shepherd who had 100 sheep, and one of them went missing. The shepherd left the ninety-nine other sheep just to go find the one missing sheep. Jesus is that shepherd, and the lost people in the world are the missing sheep. Jesus left heaven (the ninety-nine) to come to earth to find the lost people and bring them back to the herd. If Jesus loved us that much, then shouldn't we love others the same way? Shouldn't we try to imitate the shepherd in this story? Let's be more like the shepherd in this story than the older brother Henry from the previous story.

Romans 13:8-10 (NIV) says of the ten commandments, "You shall not commit adultery," "You shall not murder," "You shall not steal," "You shall not covet," and whatever other command there may be are summed up in this one command: "Love your neighbor as yourself." Love does not harm a neighbor. Therefore, love is the fulfillment of the law.

Jesus showed us through His example and His parables how to love. Jesus walked on this earth and showed everyone love. He didn't just show the rich and highly connected people love. He loved those that were sick. He loved those that were caught in adultery. He loved those that were drunk. He loved those who turned away from him for a time but came back and repented. Jesus showed us who our neighbors are. Once we catch onto how to love the way Jesus loved, we can then become the light in this dark world.

- FIVE -

What Does Jesus' Love Show Us?

J esus replied, "Love the Lord your God with all your heart and with all your soul and with all your mind" (Matt. 22:37-40 NIV). This is the first and greatest commandment. And second is like it: Love your neighbor as yourself. All the laws and the prophets hang on these two commandments.

When you first start dating someone, what do you do? How do you act? Do you put a lot of focus on that person and on that new relationship? If you are married, I probably know your answers to all of the questions. When you are starting the 'fall in love' stage with someone, you will put a lot of your time, energy, and resources into them. You will be on your best behavior. You will put more focus on your love interest than you will on your friends. You spend more of your energy on your love interest because you want to receive the same affection that you give out.

Let's ask the same questions about when you first gave your life to Jesus. When you first became a follower of Jesus, what did you do? How did you act? Did you put a lot of time, energy, and resources into Jesus and your relationship with him? I was a younger child when I asked Jesus into my heart, but I remember that I wanted to learn more about Jesus and God. When I was a teenager, I started to work on having a closer relationship with Jesus. I knew what it was like to have a relationship with a girl, and I knew I needed a closer relationship with Jesus. So, in my teenage years, I started reading the Bible more, I was attending church multiple times on Sundays and again on Wednesdays. I was also serving in the church. I set my attention on Jesus and the relationship I had with him. I didn't want to be a lukewarm Christian like it says in Revelation 3:15 (NIV), "I know your deeds, that you are neither cold nor hot. I wish you were either one or the other! So, because you are lukewarm, neither hot nor cold, I am about to spit you out of my mouth."

The first commandment that God gave Moses was that there was to be no other god before him (Exod.us 20:3). Before Moses died, he shared more wisdom with the people of Israel. He told them to love God with all their heart, soul, and mind. He also told them that they needed to relay this to their children, their children's children, and so on (Deut. 32:46). He wanted to impress this upon the heart of all the generations of Israel. We see throughout the Old Testament that the commands were impressed on the minds of his people many generations later. When Jesus was on the earth. he was tested by the leaders of the law and they asked him what the greatest commandment was. Jesus replied saying, "Love the Lord your God with all your heart, with all your soul, and with all your mind. And second to that is to love your neighbor as yourself" (Matt. 22:37-39).

The first part of the greatest commandment is to love the Lord your God with all your heart. No, God is not interested in you loving him with all four chambers of your blood-pumping muscle. Our heart symbolizes the emotional part of our being. When we say I love you to our spouse, we are showing them love as an emotion. We are saying that I am emotionally into you right now. How do we love God with our emotions? We show love through our actions toward others. When I think about how people will know we are Christians, I think of the song, "They will know we are Christians by our love." One of the simplest things we can do to show God's love is to smile at others. A smile is infectious in a good way. A simple smile and a sincere "Hello, how is your day going?" will go a long way. I do that every time I go to the grocery store to shop. I can't say how many times I have gotten a smile back or a thank you. Another good verse about loving God is Luke 10:26-28 (NIV) which states, "What is written in the law? And how do you read it? Love the Lord your God with all your heart and with all your soul and with all your strength and with all your mind and love your neighbor as yourself."

The second part of that commandment is to love the Lord our God with all your soul. The soul is the part of us that will go up to heaven when these dirty sinful bodies leave this earth. How do we love God with our souls? How do we have a relationship with God that will strengthen our bond with God? We need to communicate with God. Relationships are a two-way street. After every service, our pastor will give an invitation to the crowd to invite Jesus into their heart. After that invitation, he always says that we should try to read one chapter of the Bible every day. Do you think this is just for the fun of it? No, it's because reading God's Word is what draws us closer to him. That is one of the ways that he communicates with us. Psalms 119:11 (NIV) says that His Word we should hide in our hearts, so we won't sin against him. I truly believe that we should be feeding our souls daily. If we have ten minutes in the day to fill our minds with the stuff that is on television, then we should easily have ten minutes to dig deep into the Bible. I have a full-time job, a wife, and three young kids at home. So, I get up every morning at 5:30 a.m. so that I have time to spend at least thirty minutes with the Lord in reading His Word and talking to him through prayer. When I am feeding my soul and my mind with His Word, I am showing him that my soul is longing for him. Your time may not be at 5:30 a.m., but it's important to find time to commune with the Lord every day.

The third part of the commandment is to love the Lord with all our minds. Let me ask you a question, does what we let into our mind affect all parts of our lives? If we watch junk on television, will that junk get burned into our minds? If we listen to junk on the radio, will that junk get burned into our minds? There is a saying, "The amount of use you get out of something is determined by the quality of the item." The same can be said about what we watch and listen to. How can we love God with our mind if we are filling it with junk? We need to be intentional about what we are allowing ourselves to let come into our eyes and ears. I am reminded of a story that a great woman of God told me. It's about how beautiful a skunk is. From a distance, they look so majestic and beautiful. The black fur with the white strip going down the middle is so adorable. But if you get too close to them, or start playing with them, you will start to smell like them. In the same way, that is how the world and our media, music, and lifestyles are. They look good on the surface. They don't seem that harmful when you are at a distance. But when you start putting the world's images in your mind, the world's songs in your mind, and start taking part in its lifestyle, you start to think, talk, and see things by the world's standards. We need to have a mind that is focused on Jesus and His purpose for us.

Jesus talked many times about our worth to him. Luke 15:4-6 talks about the parable about the lost sheep. The shepherd would leave the ninety-nine sheep in the flock just to find the one that was missing. Jesus is showing us how precious we are to him. If that isn't a good enough example of how Jesus views us, then what about the fact that God created us in His image? Do you think that God would make you in His image and not think you are special? Jesus also told a parable about a merchant looking for a perfect pearl. The merchant sold everything he had and bought it. You, my friend, are that pearl! I am that pearl! Jesus is the merchant, and the value that he puts on us is far more than we could ever imagine. Another illustration is the parable about a priceless treasure found in a field. A man finds priceless treasure. He buries it again and then sells all he has and buys that field. Once again, we are that priceless treasure, and Jesus is the man who purchases the field.

We need to learn to love ourselves before we can truly love others. Like so many of you, I, too, have had many times in my life when I have struggled with loving myself. I have been affected by the words that others have said to me. I have been affected by the way that others have treated me. I have been affected by the guilt or shame I have felt when I have screwed up and done the wrong thing for the hundredth time. At those times when I am feeling down on myself, I remember what my value is to God. We all have the same value in God's eyes. Our value to God is more than you or I could ever earn. He values us so much that he gave His son's life for us. If you are like me and you have struggled with loving yourself from time to time, please know that you are precious to God. When I was struggling with loving myself, I found comfort, strength, and encouragement through the following scriptures:

> Genesis 1:26 (NIV): "Then God said, 'Let us make mankind in our image, in our likeness, so that they may rule over the fish in the sea and the birds in the sky, over the livestock and all the wild animals, and over all creatures that move along the ground.'"

> Psalm 139:13-17 (NIV): "For you created my inmost being, you knit me together in my mother's womb. I praise you because I am fearfully and wonderfully made; your works are wonderful; I know that full well. My frame was not hidden from you when I was made in the secret place when I was woven together in the depths of the earth. Your eyes saw my unformed body, all the days ordained for me were written in your book before one of them came to be. How precious to me are your thoughts, God! How vast is the sum of them!"

Psalms 40:1-2 (NIV): "I waited patiently for the Lord; he turned to me and heard my cry. He lifted me out of the slimy pit, out of the mud and mire; he set my feet on a rock and gave me a firm place to stand."

Romans 5:8 (ESV): "But God shows His love to us in that while we were still sinners, Christ died for us."

Jeremiah 29:11 (NIV): "For I know the plans I have for you," declares the Lord, "plans to prosper you and not to harm you, plans to give you hope and a future."

Ephesians 2:4-9 (NIV): "But because of His great love for us, God, who is rich in mercy, made us alive with Christ even when we were dead in transgressions – it is by grace you have been saved. And God raised us up with Christ and seated us with him in the heavenly realms in Christ Jesus, in order that in the coming ages he might show the incomparable riches of His grace, expressed in His kindness to us in Christ Jesus. For it is by grace you have been saved, through faith – and this is not from yourselves, it is the gift of God – not by works, so that no one can boast."

Matthew 10:28-31 (NIV): "Do not be afraid of those who kill the body but cannot kill the soul. Rather, be afraid of the one who can destroy both soul and body in hell. Are not two sparrows sold for a penny? Yet not one of them will fall to the ground outside your father's care. And even the very hairs of your head are all numbered. So don't be afraid; you are worth more than many sparrows."

Luke 12:6-7 (NIV): "Are not five sparrows sold for two pennies? Yet not one of them is forgotten by God. Indeed, the very hairs of your head are all numbered. Don't be afraid; you are worth more than many sparrows."

Titus 3:4-7 (NIV): "But when the kindness and love of God our Savior appeared, he saved us, not because of righteous things we had done, but because of His mercy. He saved us through the washing of rebirth and renewal by the Holy Spirit, whom he poured out on us generously through Jesus Christ our Savior, so that, having been justified by His grace, we might become heirs having the hope of eternal life."

You are worth more than you can even fathom. God loves you even when you feel unlovable. God loves you even when you feel hopeless. God loves you even when you feel lost. Just look up to Him and ask Him to draw near to you.

I am reminded of the poem "Footprints" by Margaret Fishback Powers. There is a poster with a picture of one set of footprints in the sand. The poem basically said that through life, there will be many times when you will see two sets of footprints. Those are when Jesus is walking beside you. When you see only one set of footprints, that is when you are weak and weary, when your heart aches. That is when Jesus is carrying you.

Before we can truly love the way God intended us to love, we must make sure we love God and that we are loving ourselves. We need to make sure there is no hatred in our hearts. We need to forgive those who have harmed us. If we still hold anger, pain, or resentment towards another then we can't fully love like Christ. In Luke 6:39-42 (NIV) Jesus shares this wisdom:

> Can the blind lead the blind? Will they not both fall into a pit? The student is not above the teacher, but everyone who is fully trained will be like their teacher. Why do you look at the speck of sawdust in your brother's eye and pay no attention to the plank in your own eye? How can you say to your brother, "Brother, let me take the speck out of your eye when you yourself fail to see the plank in your own eye? You hypocrite, first take the plank out of your eye, and then you will see clearly to remove the speck from your brother's eye."

God's word shows how to love, and we see examples of how to love others. Love will take the plank from our own eyes and help us not to see the speck in others' eyes. We will feel the compassion of Christ pouring out of us onto those who need Christ.

This piece of wisdom can be applied to so many things in life, but I challenge you to apply it to unforgiveness. How can you give love when you have hatred in your heart? How can you give love when you have anger toward another in your heart? How can you love when you have resentment? You can't. It's just like the plank in your eye. The unforgiveness in your heart is like a blindfold over your eyes. It blinds you from seeing real love. We first have to forgive others and give the offenses to God. Second, we should pray to God, and ask him for help with showing forgiveness to the person who hurt us. Once you forgive and give it to God then you will be able to forget about the offense and go on with peace in your heart. When you can do that then you can truly be a good student and learn from the teacher (Jesus).

How do you know how to read? How do you know how to write? How do you know how to do your job? How does a doctor know how to take care of their patient? If you are married, how do you know how to love your spouse? If you own a pet, how do you know how to take care of it? All of these questions have the same answer. You were taught. Someone modeled how to do those things. If you went to college or trade school then you studied and learned to prepare yourself for your job or career. Doctors know how to take care of their patients by being taught by a teacher or another doctor. If you are married, you more than likely learned how to love your spouse by watching your parents, grandparents, or guardians. The same with the pet. We learn by observing and putting into practice what we see. We try to mimic what is being modeled. That is how we learn to love others.

Jesus was and is the ultimate teacher. We should mimic what he modeled. Jesus cared about every person he came into contact with, even those that didn't like him. While Jesus was on earth, he invested His time into the people he came into contact with. We need to invest in the people we come in contact with. When I say invest, I'm not necessarily talking about money. By listening to the Holy Spirit and following his prompts, we can influence those around us. If he asks you to help a lady cross the street, you help the lady cross the street. If he asks you to hold to door open and smile at the couple going into the store behind you, then you open the door and smile at them. If he asks you to give a person on the street shoes, then do it. We don't know what the impact of investing in others has on them. That one smile might have broken up an intense moment the couple was having. It might have made them forget about why they were upset with one another.

Here is a fun little story about just this. I was on vacation with my wife and during this vacation, my heart was hurting for the people I saw around me. The people weren't sick or homeless or anything horrible. My heart just hurt for them because I could tell they were spiritually lost. I could tell they didn't know God's love. My spirit was heightened to an awareness of the needs of the people around me. I was walking around the city like I normally do when I am in a city I don't know or a city that would be fun to explore. My wife, on the other hand, was relaxing back at the hotel. While I was walking, I saw a lot of different people. People-watching while exploring a new place is fun for me. What started as entertainment, turned to sadness as I saw a gentleman walking around with ragged clothes and no shoes. It broke my heart. I lost track of him, and I didn't see him for the rest of that day. Later that day, I told my wife about the man and how I was struck by him. The next day I was out exploring again, and I saw the man. He was in the same clothes and still not wearing shoes. We were in a hot city. I believe the temperature was in the mid '80s. There is no way that his feet were not burning. I was again drawn to him, and then I heard the Holy Spirit tell me to help the man. At times, I struggle to listen and follow the Holy Spirit, however, I am trying to listen and follow more. I went to a store and bought a pair of sandals for the man. Again, I lost track of him for a few minutes, but then found him. I took the shoes over to him and told him that God wanted him to have them. He smiled and told me thanks. I'm pretty sure he would have been smiling no matter if I brought the shoes to him or not (he was high), but that was not the point. The point was that I listened to the Holy Spirit, and I invested in the person He told me to invest into. I don't know that man's story, but I do know that man is a child of God. He is precious in God's eyes, so he is precious to me. God believes that man's feet were precious, so he told me to get shoes so they would be covered.

While I was on that same vacation, I used my 5:30 a.m. time with God to walk and sit next to the ocean to have time with God. While watching God's beauty in the ocean, listening to the waves hitting the shore, God told me that all that beauty is designed by Him. It is designed by His Holiness, and each person on this earth is created by God's holiness. We need to see the beauty in everyone. And I'm not talking about a perfect jawline or a perfectly shaped physique. Yes, people hold beauty on the outside but I am talking about the beauty we need to see on the inside of everyone we meet. If there isn't much beauty on the inside, that means that they have been hurt and they don't know God's love.

If we see someone whose inner beauty isn't as bright (someone who has been hurt because they haven't surrendered to God), should we just walk away and say that person isn't salvageable? If someone is pushing us away, do we just take the push and go? No, if someone is pushing you away, it's likely because they were hurt. Hurt people hurt people. There is something inside of them that has been hurt, and they don't know how to heal from that hurt. But you and I know what can mend their heart. We know what can heal their hurt. It is the love of Jesus. We need to love that person even more so.

There will be times when we are called by God to love a person. I call these divine appointments. These are supernatural appointments set up by God as opportunities to breathe life and love into their situations. God will ask us to do something kind for a person. God may ask us to talk with a person. We are asked by God to plant His seeds into people. We are the ones who plant the seeds. We are the gardener, and we need to remember this. We plant the seeds, or maybe we water the seeds that were planted. Maybe we will nourish the seeds (by a kind word or action), but ultimately, it is up to that person (that we put the seed into) to allow that seed to grow. We can't save people, but we aren't to condemn people either. It is God's job to do both. I think there are times we think that we can be a person's savior. We can't save anyone. We can't even save ourselves. Jesus is the only one who can save us. A friend of friend of mine back in high school found Jesus and got saved. He was on fire for Jesus. He would try to witness to people, but if they wouldn't listen, so he would condemn them. That left a bad taste in a lot of people's mouths. I know his intentions were good, but he didn't realize that he was being judgmental of people. We are called to witness and spread the good news of Jesus to people. We aren't called to condemn them if they don't repent right there.

On my vacation, I could have judged the guy that was barefoot. The man was higher than a kite, but I was still moved with love towards the man. God asked me to give the man sandals not to give him judgment. On my vacation, I could have been judgmental to all the people I saw who were dressed scantily clad, but instead, my heart was hurting for them, and I had compassion for them.

With Christ in our hearts, we are to love the people of the world, not be of the world. I am not supposed to judge people who do not share my viewpoints, but I am supposed to love them. I am not supposed to treat people with hatred, I am supposed to love them. I am not supposed to follow the crowd, but I am supposed to love them. We are called to love others. Let us do that by following Christ's examples. Let us do that by listening to the Holy Spirit and following the call He gives us. Let us do that by being non-judgmental towards others.

We are called to love God, love ourselves, love others, and love our family. I have to admit that this is a hard one for me. I grew up in a loving family, and I had parents who were both involved in our lives. They have been married for over 50 years now. Growing up, there was a lot of fighting in our house. Mainly the fighting was between me and my sisters. There was no doubt that we loved each other and there was no doubt that we had each other's backs. It's just we were emotional a lot of the time. So, growing up in a family with strong German roots and mix in five kids who fought a lot leaves you with a distorted view of a loving family.

I had a couple of friends that lived up the street from me with whom I spent a lot of time with as a kid. It was at their houses that I got to see how other families interacted. I can relate to the family dynamics of Joseph (Gen. 37:50). Joseph was his father's favorite son, and his 11 brothers knew it. Joseph's brothers were jealous of him, so they sold him into slavery. But, at the end of the story, Joseph is the one who saved his family. So, even if you come from an emotionally charged family, God can and will use you for His kingdom.

Next to God, our family should be the ones that we love the most. But if we are honest with ourselves, this can be difficult. I believe we are hardest on the ones we are closest to. This is not the way that God wants family dynamics to be. I was raised with the following belief, and I still believe this to be true. God first, marriage second, kids/family third, and ministry/others forth. This is the order that we are to love. God should always be first. He sent Jesus (who is God in the flesh) to die so we could be in fellowship with him. Our spouse is second on the tier of our love. After all, if we didn't love our spouse, then we wouldn't have our children. Our children, parents, siblings, grandparents, etc. are the next tier down. The fourth tier of love should be for others.

Now that we have mapped out the hierarchy, what does love in our family look like? I think it depends on your role in the family. As the man of the family, the way I love looks different from my wife. As a man, love looks like putting your wife and kids before yourself. God called men to serve their families just as Christ served his church. A simple example would be, I always make sure that my wife and kids have their food on the table before my own; it's just one of many ways you can demonstrate a servant's heart. In John 13:13-17 (NIV), Jesus is talking to His disciples after he finished washing their feet. He says, "You call me 'Teacher' and 'Lord,' and rightly so, for that is what I am. Now that I, your Lord, and Teacher, have washed your feet, you also should wash one another's feet. I have set you an example that you should do as I have done for you. Very truly I tell you, no servant is greater than His master, nor is a messenger greater than the one who sent him. Now that you know these things, you will be blessed if you do them." Jesus' example is simple, beautiful, and a profound depiction of how to treat our family. The disciples were brothers. They were a family, and Jesus told them that they should serve one another. Not one of the disciples was more important than the others. If we want to be good leaders in our family, then we should first be the best servant in the family.

Another way men can show love is by spiritually leading their families. I believe that God made the husband the spiritual leader in the family. Ephesians 5:22-28 (NIV) states:

> Wives, submit yourselves to your own husbands as you do to the Lord. For the husband is the head of the wife, as Christ is the head of the church, His body, of which he is the Savior. Now as the church submits to Christ, so also wives should submit to their husbands in everything. Husbands, love your, wives, just as Christ loved the church and gave himself up for her to make her holy, cleansing her by the washing with water through the Word and to present her to himself as a radiant church without stain or wrinkle or any other blemish, but holy and blameless. In this same way, husbands ought to love their wives as their own bodies. He who loves his wife loves himself.

Unfortunately, these verses are often taken out of context and distorted. But husbands are to be servants to their wives, and husbands are to give of themselves for their wives. Men, we should be loving our wives in the same way that Jesus loves His church. We are called to be servants to our families. Be the head of the family spiritually just like Jesus is the head of the church spiritually. Be willing to give of yourselves for your wives. Be kind and caring to your kids.

My wife, who is a very strong woman, sums up the role of a wife in the family as the wife in Proverbs 31:10-12 (NIV) which says, "A wife of noble character who can find? She is worth far more than rubies. Her husband has full confidence in her and lacks nothing of value. She brings him good, not harm, all the days of her life." Proverbs 31:20-30 (NIV) says,

She opens her arms to the poor and extends her hands to the needy. When it snows, she has no fear for her household; for all of them are clothed in scarlet. She makes coverings for her bed; she is clothed in fine linen and purple. Her husband is respected at the city gate, where he takes his seat among the elders of the land. She makes linen garments and sells them and supplies the merchants with sashes. She is clothed with strength and dignity; she can laugh at the days to come. She speaks with wisdom and faithful instruction is on her tongue. She watches over the affairs of her household and does not eat the bread of idleness. Her children arise and call her blessed; her husband also and praises her: "Many women do noble things, but you surpass them all." Charm is deceptive, and beauty is fleeting, but a woman who fears the Lord is to be praised.

A loving wife brings about confidence in her husband. She is someone who helps her husband have joy in all of his life. She is willing to help any family member when the time arises. She is nurturing to her children. She is caring for her children; she will make sure they are well taken care of. She always speaks life to whomever she is talking with.

For those who are not married, what does loving one another look like? The traits look the same as those of the husband and wife. We all should have a servant's heart towards others. We should be willing to give of ourselves for the sake of another. We should be caring for the needs of others. Love is nonjudgmental and respectful. Love does not treat someone meanly if they are not living the way we think they should. Love will also shine even when we do not agree with someone else's opinion. Love is uplifting. So, what does a loving family look like? Simply put, a loving family emulates Christ's love for the church.

- SIX -

How Do We Practice Christ's Love Toward Others?

Practicing Christ's love should be a simple thing to do, but for most of us, it's not. We have this thing called flesh that fights with our spirit. Paul explains this in Romans 7: 14-18 (NIV):

> We know that the law is spiritual, but I am unspiritual, sold as a slave to sin. I do not understand what I do. For what I want to do I do not do, but what I hate I do. And if I do what I do not want to do, I agree that the law is good. As it is, it is no longer I, myself, who do it, but it is sin living in me. For I know that good itself does not dwell in me, that is, in my sinful nature (my flesh). For I have the desire to do what is good, but I cannot carry it out.

Paul is saying that the flesh and the spirit are constantly fighting. But through Jesus, we have conquered our flesh. And if we have conquered the flesh and the sinful nature of this body, then we can be more like Jesus. When we are saved, it's not like a switch is turned on and we are no longer earthly or sinful. No, we still have that sinful flesh, but now we have God's grace in our life. How do we fight the flesh? We can't fight it alone. We need God's grace and we need the helper. The helper is the Holy Spirit, and what a helper is he.

What would happen if we started to see people the way that Jesus sees them? How would we act toward them? How would we treat them? What type of words would we use? What type of attitude would we have when we are around them? These are all good questions that we should ask ourselves every time we don't feel like being loving. I also believe these are good questions to ask ourselves every day. If we see people the way Jesus sees them, then our hearts would be different. Our hearts would be full of compassion, joy, love, and sometimes sadness. Compassionate enough to do something for them. Joyful enough to spread happy words to them. We would be loving in our actions towards others and we would feel a sense of sadness when we see their hurt. Let's look at a few tips that I use to put Jesus' love into practice.

The first thing we have to do to practice Jesus' love is to follow His example. In Chapter Three, I gave you different examples of how Jesus showed love. I am not going to repeat those ways, but I will simply say that if we want to be good at something, we need to follow the instructions. Jesus' instruction manual is the Bible. More specifically, I am talking about the Gospels. We need to read through the Gospels to see how Jesus loved others while on earth. When I am struggling with how to fix something I always look for the instructions or watch someone who is a professional to see how they fix it. When my wife's vehicle had bad brakes on it, I knew how to fix it. The reason I knew how to replace the brakes (and rotors) on her vehicle is that as a kid I had the opportunity to watch my father change car brakes several times. That will happen when you have six people in the house that are all driving at the same time; you will have many vehicles to repair. I studied my father when he changed the brakes. I even got to watch and help friends that needed to change their vehicle's brakes. The reason I knew how to replace the brakes on my wife's vehicle is that I had followed the instructions I learned from my father.

Another example happened tonight before I sat down to write. I put landscaping lights on our deck to give us light in the backyard. I got the light out and I grabbed the instructions that came with them. I glanced over them but I didn't use them. Fast forward an hour and a half, and it's dark outside. Guess what? The lights were not working. If I would have read the instructions instead of glancing at them, I would have noticed that I needed to push a small button on the bottom of the lights to turn them on. When we only glance over the Word of God, we might miss information we need to know from Jesus. We need to read with the intent of learning from God. With loving, it should be the same thing. We should practice what we are taught by Jesus in the Bible.

The next thing we should do is listen to the Holy Spirit. Jesus said in John 16:7 (NIV) "But very truly I tell you, it is for your good that I am going away. Unless I go away, the Advocate will not come to you; but if I go, I will send him to you." What is an advocate? It is someone that will plead the cause of another. So, if the Holy Spirit is an advocate for us, that means he will help us with our needs. The

Holy Spirit is our advocate, and he is our helper. He will help us when we need help. He will guide us when we need guidance. What do we do when we need someone to help us with something? We go to someone we trust who will give us good advice. We listen to them since they know what to do. In school, did you listen to your teacher when they taught you algebra? If you know what X + Y = Z means, then I would say you listened.

The Holy Spirit is the same as a teacher. He wants to show us the way when we ask him how to do it. We need to learn to listen to the Holy Spirit. He normally doesn't speak in an audible voice (at least in my experience). When he speaks to me, I can feel it in my soul. There are many times that I have felt him speaking to me about others. He knows what others need, and he knows who is best suited for helping them. He knows how others want to be treated, and he knows who is best suited to treat them well. So, if you are ever at the store, and you feel like something inside your soul is telling you to pay for the elderly couple's groceries, that is the Holy Spirit gently nudging you to show that couple some love. Once I was driving down the road, when I felt like I needed to help someone. A quarter mile down the road there was a lady on the side of the road. I found out she was almost out of gas, and she needed to get to her daughter's house to watch her grandchild. I gave her the twenty-dollar bill I had. I got back in my vehicle and drove off. Not once did I question if she was telling me the truth or not. I was just happy that I heard the voice of the Holy Spirit and that I listened to him.

Do you like it when someone lets you go before them in a line? Do you like it when someone opens a door for you? Do you like when all the lights you go through while driving are green? I am going to venture out and say you answered yes to all of those questions. We like when we are treated kindly by others. I don't know anyone who doesn't. We can practice Jesus' love by treating others the way he would or when we treat others kindly. Jesus treated us like we were royalty. He gave himself as a sacrifice for us. I'm not saying that we need to give our lives for another person. I'm saying that if we are followers of Jesus, then we should follow His example of love. We should treat others like they matter to us. We should treat others like they mean more to us than our selfish desires. We should treat others as if they are a piece of gold. Treat them like they are valuable. Because they are more valuable than gold to Jesus.

Have you ever heard the phrase "You can talk the talk, but can you walk the walk?" The phrase means that words are good, but action is better. I grew up in Missouri and growing up, I learned that the state's nickname is "The show me state." I grew up wondering why you would want that type of nickname. But the older I got, the more I understood that I liked to know how to do stuff. I wanted to be shown what to do instead of just being told how to do something. It's not that I wasn't smart enough to figure it out on my own, it's that I liked to learn from someone who already knew how to do it. I liked to learn by watching the actions of others. I also learned that my actions were very meaningful to others. When it comes to loving others, it is more meaningful to do things for them than to just say nice things. Don't get me wrong, nice words are necessary. Our actions just mean so much more. Let's take the story I used earlier about the Holy Spirit prompting me to pull over to help the lady who was running low on gas. Do you think it would have had the same impact on her if I had just slowed down, said some nice and kind words to her, and then driven away? No, she would have wondered why I stopped in the first place if I wasn't planning on trying to help her. The action of pulling over, getting out of my vehicle, and talking with her to find out what she needed probably had a great impact. The fact that I gave her money probably had an even greater impact. Another example is with a lady from our church who is a widow. She had made a comment to my wife about needing help with yard work. What has the greater impact on her, telling her that I enjoy doing yard work? Or me going over to the lady's house and helping her with the yard work that her husband would have normally done? It would be more impactful for me to do the work.

When I talk about doing a service for others, I'm talking about doing it selflessly. I'm talking about taking action to help others in love without expecting anything in return. I can remember as a kid my dad would learn about elderly neighbors who needed yard work done. He would send me over to their houses to have me do the yard work for them. I never got paid, and it's not that they didn't offer to pay either. My dad was trying to show me that we do things for others out of love, not just for money. That is what Christ did for us, so that is what we should do for others. This didn't happen only once, it happened multiple times. And a lot of the time, my dad would be there helping me. I grew up in a house where I was taught at a young age that you put others before yourself and that you show them you care. Once again, I think Jesus proved this with His sacrifice on the cross, that actions speak louder than words. So next time you see someone that needs help, don't just think in your head that someone else will help, no, you need to think about how you can help. God placed you in that place with that person for a reason. Our actions, good or bad, will reflect on how people see Jesus.

Another way that we can practice Christ's love is to have a vision of how we can bless others. During Jesus' ministry, there were many examples of how he blessed others, and those blessings took on many forms. One example was His first miracle as reported in John 2:1-10 (NIV):

> On the third day a wedding took place at Cana in Galilee. Jesus' mother was there, and Jesus and His disciples had also been invited to the wedding. When the wine was gone, Jesus' mother said to him, "They have no more wine." "Woman, why do you involve me?" Jesus replied. "My hour has not yet come." His mother said to the servants, "Do whatever he tells you." Nearby stood six stone water jars, the kind used by the Jews for ceremonial washing, each holding from twenty to thirty gallons. Jesus said to the servants, "Fill the jars with water" so, they filled them to the brim. Then he told them, "Now draw some out and take it to the master of the banquet." They did so, and the master of the banquet tasted the water that had been turned into wine. He did not realize where it had come from, though the servants who had

drawn the water knew. Then he called the bridegroom aside and said, "Everyone brings out the choice wine first and then the cheaper wine after the guests have had too much to drink, but you have saved the best till now."

Jesus used His first sign of being Christ to bless a couple who got married. Another example is He blessed a royal official by healing his dying son (John 4:43-54). This was Jesus' second sign that he performed after starting His ministry. Jesus blessed over 5,000 people by feeding them with the five fish and two loaves of bread that were given to him by a boy (Matt. 14:16-21). I could go on and on with a long list of all the times that Jesus blessed people. If you read the Gospels, you will see that most of the Gospels are about Jesus' ministry and the different ways people were blessed. Jesus' vision of how he could bless others was His ministry. The end game of why Jesus came to this earth was to bless the human race. Even on the cross, Jesus blessed people. A thief was hanging next to him, and the thief believed that Jesus was Christ the Messiah, and he told Jesus so. Jesus told the man that he would be in paradise with him that day. On the cross and with the cross, he blessed us. He tore the barrier that sin put up by dying on that cross.

In what ways can we bless others? What is your vision on how to bless others? What gifts or talents do you have that you can use to bless others? What means do you have to bless others? I could go on, and on with questions about blessing others. When I talk about blessing others I am not necessarily talking about money. I think one way that we can bless others is in the area that we have been blessed in. So, if you have been over abundantly blessed with a green thumb, then you could take some of the fruits and vegetables you grew to the local homeless shelter or food bank. Or, if it's flowers that you are good at growing, you could take bouquets to your local nursing homes. What a blessing it would be to the residents that live there. If you have been blessed with mechanical skills then you could give your services free to single mothers or fathers. You could perform oil changes for those poor college students that are going to college in your community. If you love dogs, you could volunteer at the local humane society or you could volunteer to take some of your elderly neighbors' dogs for walks. If you have the skills to cut hair or do makeup, you could volunteer at the local women's shelter to show the women there some love by doing their hair or makeup. There are many ways we can bless people. If you have the monetary means, you could donate your money to worthy causes. I heard of a man in Kansas who would dress up like Santa Clause at Christmas time and stand outside the local Walmart handing out hundred-dollar bills to the people who looked like they needed a little holiday cheer. This man is being a blessing to others.

Maybe your vision to help others is by giving time. Are you good at yard work? Are you a good listener? Do you have lonely single elderly neighbors? Do you know of any elderly people at a nursing home who don't have family near them? Earlier in the chapter, I talked about how as a teenager, my dad would volunteer me to do yardwork for neighbors. I would do that without expecting anything in return. In James 1:26-27 (NIV), we are told how to treat our widows and orphans. Verse 27 states, "Religion that God our Father accepts as pure and faultless is this: to look after orphans and widows in their distress and to keep oneself from being polluted by the world."

A few years ago, we lived next door to three elderly sisters. When we moved into our house, there was no landscaping at their house. The sister and my family shared an ugly junction box that sat on both our properties. My wife and I didn't like how it looked, so we considered putting landscaping around the box and other parts of our yard. We talked with our lovely neighbors about the junction box and our landscaping ideas. They told us that they had the same thought about it, but had never got around to planting anything. So, we agreed that we would landscape around the box on both of our properties. They asked to pay for the plants that would be on their property. We agreed with that, but my wife, kids, and I were the ones who did the work. The sisters wanted to pay us for doing the landscaping but we refused. We were more than happy to do the work on their property for nothing. That was just one of the ways we blessed them. My full-time job is in the IT world, and our neighbors knew that. So, when they would need computer help, I would go over and help them. I would refuse to take any money when they offered because I enjoyed helping them out, and I enjoyed blessing them. I was able to use my God-given talents to be a blessing to them.

Maybe one of the ways that we have envisioned loving others is by giving to others. I already talked about giving our time and energy to others to show Jesus' love to others, but what if we have the means to give monetarily to others? I know not everyone has the means to give money to others. I know the times that I do give to others monetarily, it is times that the Holy Spirit has urged me to.

I took different business courses in college and most of them had a common theme. You take care of the bills of the business and then take care of yourself. This is also a common theme when you talk with financial gurus about personal finances. They say that you should make sure you pay your bills, but you also pay yourself. Most people will call that their "mad" money. The money you set aside for your daily coffee or your soda. The money is set aside for that new video game or a night at the movies. Whatever we call it, we all have that money we feel like we deserve to spend on ourselves. I agree that if we are working hard for our money, we should enjoy our life. But I have also found something else that brings joy to my life, and that is listening to the Holy Spirit about giving money to others that need it. I remember a time I was running a few errands to grab a couple of items we needed for dinner that night. Turning into the shopping center, I saw a person standing at a stop light with a sign. As soon as I saw the person, I felt the Holy Spirit speak to me on the inside about giving that person some food. While shopping, I grabbed a sandwich and a bottle of water so I could give them to the person. I spent more money on the person than on the two grocery items I needed. After I handed her the food, I felt great.

It feels great when we can give to others. I know not everyone has extra money to just give to others, but what if we had a spot in our budgets that was "MAD" money or what I like to call "Making a Difference" money? I know that we are told to tithe to the church, and I fully support that. I think that all believers should be giving a tithe to God. I am simply saying that another way to show Christ's love is to give freely. I'm not saying you have to give money to every person you see. I'm saying we need to listen to the Holy Spirit about who to give it to. He will also guide you to give a certain amount. I have more examples of how listening to the Holy Spirit has prompted me to give money away. Money that I didn't even miss once it left my hands. There was a time when I was on my way to pick up my kids from daycare. I saw a lady standing next to her car on the side of the road. I felt the Holy Spirit telling me to stop and help her. She had stopped to visit someone, and she was worried about how she was going to get home because her car was empty, and she didn't have any money for gas. I had a twenty-dollar bill in my wallet, so I gave it to her. I choose to believe her because the Holy Spirit prompted me to help her.

There was a time a few summers ago that my wife and I were in our backyard doing yardwork while the kids were playing. My wife said that while praying the night before, she felt the Holy Spirit leading her to give a person we knew $500 dollars. That was a lot of money for us to just give away, but when she told me that, I knew she was right. I felt a peace in my spirit about the nudging from the Holy Spirit she got. We gave the person the money, and we later found out that she needed that exact amount of money for a car repair. Not in any one of those occurrences did we ever feel like we missed the money. We have always been just fine financially every time the Holy Spirit told us to give money to someone. I'm not suggesting you make your "MAD" money a huge amount, but I am warning you that if you do start giving money to those in need, you will feel the Joy of the Lord. It might even make you want to give more. I have heard of countless times when people have either given money to others or they have received the money. In our community, the Christian radio station promotes doing the "drive-thru difference" where on a certain day of the week and week of the month, they promote others to pay for the meal of the person that is behind them in the drive-thru. I heard how when one person starts, that it catches on like wildfire. I heard that it lasted at one fast food drive-thru for over two hours. Two hours of people paying for the food of the person behind them.

Just think about how much of an impact you could make on someone if you tried this. I know when you barely have enough money to get by it will seem scary. But that is when God challenges us. He wants us to rely on him for everything. So, if he urges us to give the ten dollars that we have in our purse to the person in line behind us at the store, then go out on faith and do it. You will see how different you feel. You will not worry about the ten dollars. You will probably forget about the ten dollars. I know every time that I have done this, I have not once worried about the money that I gave away.

This last section we will be dealing with is how we are supposed to love others by letting our actions be led by our emotions. Believe it or not, Jesus did get emotional when it came to people. I think the two best examples are when Jesus' close friend Lazarus died. Jesus wept. Jesus knew that he would bring Lazarus back to life, but his human side showed emotions. Jesus wept because of His friend's death, but after His mourning, he raised Lazarus from the dead. Another great example of Jesus being emotional was when he was dying on the cross. The very people that Jesus was hanging on the cross for (and eventually dying for) were standing around and mocking him. They had been mocking him as he carried His cross. They had been throwing rocks and food at him. They beat him. Yet on the cross, he said to His father in heaven, "Please forgive them for they know not what they are doing!"

Even on the cross, Jesus was showing His love for us. "Please forgive them for they know not what they are doing,"—those words right there showed His attitude of love for His children. We should be showing Jesus' love to people through our attitudes toward them. I know this is not an easy one for me. I do not have a very good poker face. If I am not pleased with someone, I do not have to say anything for them to know. Unfortunately, that has always been my superpower. I am sure that my attitude and/or body language (they go hand in hand) have confused people instead of bringing them closer to Christ. I have worked hard on this over the years. Even though I still don't have a good poker face, what has changed is on the inside. My heart has grown to be more compassionate toward others. So now instead of others seeing anger or sarcasm, they see the compassion on my face. This all started when I took to heart Luke 10:26-28 (NIV) which says, "What is written in the law?" Jesus replied. "How do you read it?" The man answered, 'Love the Lord your God with all your heart and with all your soul and with all your strength and with all your mind and love your neighbor as yourself.' 'You have answered correctly,' Jesus replied. 'Do this and you will live.'"

Our attitude starts with the shape of our heart is in. If we are loving God with all our heart, then there is no room for hate. If we are loving God with all our heart, then there is no room for mean words spoken. If we are loving God with all our heart, then there is no room for judgment. If we are loving God with all our heart, then there is no room for mean words written. If we are loving God with all our heart, then there is no room for mean actions toward others.

Once I figured out my attitude would change when my heart changed, everything changed for me. There are still times that I will struggle with having the correct attitude but that is when I must check my heart. It is more than likely that I missed my quiet time with God that day or I had a hard day at work and instead of taking a few moments to talk with God about the problems, I went about thinking I could fix them all on my own. By the way, that was the wrong choice. I have found more and more that when my heart is right with God and focused on God, I won't have an attitude or bad thoughts about others when they are doing something that goes against God's Word. When we are deep in love with God, we will be moved to love people the way God loves people and dislike the sin that God dislikes. We need to ask God for the compassion that he has for us. We are called not to judge anyone. God is the only one who should be judging the sins in this world. Even though He will judge each one of us, God loves ALL.

You should be loving so much that you get emotional about giving (showing) love to others. Christians who are not showing love are shopping at the wrong store. This is so true. Love and hate do not come from the same God. God who created us only knows love. Satan who is a fallen angel (and not a god) because he wanted to be God and tried to overtake God, he is the god of hate. Hate is stealing our time with God, it's stealing our closeness with God, and it's stealing our redemption in Christ. When we are unconditional with love, then we are more than conquers in Christ. The more we pour God's love into our lives, the more hate and shame will fall out of our life.

> James 1:19 (NIV): "Be quick to listen and slow to speak and slow to get angry."

> James 4:10 (NIV): "Humble yourselves before the Lord."

> 1 John 4:18 (NIV): "There is no fear in love. But perfect love drives out fear because fear has to do with punishment. The one who fears is not made perfect in love."

In Christ, we have no fear. How then can we fear things when we know in Christ that our lives are better off in Christ than in this world? Love your neighbor with the love that God has put in you. Not selfish love, but the love God has shown us through His son Jesus Christ. Jesus didn't show selfishness in the garden when he was betrayed, did he? No, he healed one of the men that accused him. He put the man's ear back in its place after Peter cut it off. On the cross, he accepted a thief's forgiveness when the thief recognized that Jesus was truly the Son of God. On the cross, Jesus could have asked the angels to take His pain, but he didn't. He took all that pain, shame, and hate on himself. That should be the definition of selflessness. As Christians, we are asked to mimic or copy Jesus Christ. God doesn't ask us to take the sins of the world on our shoulders, but he does ask us to give ourselves for our brothers and sisters. The world wants us to believe that it has the best love. We are not asked to mimic or copy the world, are we?

First John 4:8-9 (NIV) says, "Whoever does not love does not know God because God is love. This is how God showed His love among us. He sent His one and only Son into the world that we might live through him."

Those are some powerful words; if you don't love, you don't know God. What is John talking about here? Is this the wishy-washy love of the world? No, he is talking about a love that is an action. If we don't show our brothers and sisters love not only through words but also action, then we don't know God. We are to help out our fellow humans when they need it. Back in the early days of the Christian church, Christians would sell items that they had so they could help the people who were needy. Why would they do that? Because they knew if they helped others then those whom they helped would see that Jesus was truly the Son of God. They would come to know God through a personal relationship with him as it says in these three passages from 1 John:

1 John 4:15-17 (NIV): "If anyone acknowledges that Jesus is the Son of God, God lives in them and they in

79

God. And so, we know and rely on the love God has for us. God is love. Whoever lives in love lives in God and God in them. This is how love is made complete among us so that we will have confidence on the day of Judgement: In this world we are like Jesus."

1 John 4:19 (NIV): "We love because he first loved us."

1 John 4:20-21 (NIV): "Whoever claims to love God yet hates a brother or sister is a liar. For whoever does not love their brother and sister, whom they have seen, cannot love God whom they have not seen. And he has given us this command: Anyone who loves God must also love their brother and sister."

I could go on and on with scriptures that talk about loving God and loving others. Instead of giving you more examples now, I will put those at the back of the book. I encourage you to read those when you feel like you need a little help with loving yourself and loving others.

Instead of feeling judgmental about someone else's actions, I feel sorrow for them because, just like Jesus said on the cross, "They know not what they are doing." Sure, they are aware of what they are doing but they are not aware of how that affects their soul and the life they have outside of this human body. So, I cannot judge anyone for that. If they do know God and they have turned away from God, then I still can't judge because I am not God. We need to lower our expectations of others that don't know Christ. That is just it, they don't know Christ. I was in the store the other night with my young kids doing our usual grocery shopping. We were going up and down the aisles getting the food we needed for the week. My kids were being loud and goofing around. In my head, I was starting to get embarrassed because my kids weren't acting like I thought they should act. In my head, I wanted them to act like adults. I wanted them to walk alongside the cart, talk quietly, and not bother other people. That's when it dawned on me that they are acting the way they know how to act. They are acting like kids their age act. I just went about getting our groceries and gave them grace because they were only doing what they knew to do. In this same way, those who don't have a relationship with God aren't going to act the cookie-cutter way most Christians want them to act. They aren't Christians, so they won't act that way. Another group to think about with this example are new Christians. A new Christian is not going to act like a pastor or an elder in a Church. A new Christian is still learning how to get that old life out of them. The old shell of themselves can still be on a person for a little while. We need to give those people grace.

The other day I saw a sticker on the back window of a car that said, "Don't hate people, hate the disease." It got me thinking about how there is truth to that. We are not called to judge others but to love them. We don't have to love their choices because their choices aren't that of a child of God. Christ didn't care about what caused someone to be in the state they were in when they needed a miracle. He cared about where their heart was. If they truly believed that he could heal them, then they were healed. He healed the poor, the sick, the addicted, and those who were caught in transgressions. If we are supposed to be imitating Jesus, then we should be loving the poor, the sick, the addicted, and those who may have other transgressions. We shouldn't be looking at what they are doing, we should be loving them so they can come to know the one who can heal them from their sins. So, like the bumper sticker I saw, don't judge the person, love them with Christ's love. You don't have to like their sins (just like God doesn't like ours) but you do need to love them.

One way that helps me not to be judgmental is by remembering that sin is sin. What I mean by that is Jesus viewed hating your brother as the same as killing a man. He also considered lusting after another woman the same as adultery. Both these examples can be described in Matthew 5:21-30. From God's point of view, in Heaven sin looks like sin. It is a disobedient act that separates us from him. From his point of view, he sees our sins as linear. Humans view sins on a scale that is not linear. So, if we get into the mindset of our sin is the same as someone else's sin, then we won't judge others as much.

Do you remember the saying from your childhood "Sticks and stones may break my bones, but words will never hurt me!" Those words were and still are very false. Our words are like a dou-ble-edged sword. Words have the power to heal or kill others. That is why James 3:3-6 (NIV) says,

> When we put bits into the mouths of horses to make
> them obey us, we can turn the whole animal. Or take
> ships as an example. Although they are so large and

are driven by strong winds, they are steered by a very small rudder wherever the pilot wants to go. Likewise, the tongue is a small part of the body, but it makes great boasts. Consider when a great forest is set on fire by a small spark. The tongue also is a fire, a world of evil among the parts of the body. It corrupts the whole body, sets the whole course of one's life on fire, and is itself set on fire by hell.

God loves us even when we are a hot mess. He doesn't ask or need us to clean up before coming to him. Second Corinthians 10: 3-5 (NIV) says:

For though we live in the world, we do not wage war as the world does. The weapons we fight with are not the weapons of the world. On the contrary, they have the divine power to demolish strongholds. We demolish arguments and every pretension that sets itself up against the knowledge of God, and we take captive every thought to make it obedient to Christ.

We may live in this world but the way we live should not be the same as those people that believe in the world's ruler. So, if this world is telling us to dress the way they dress, should we? If the world tells us that we should use the same vulgar words it uses, should we? If the world tells us to view each other people as objects, should we? The answer is no, not because some religious group says so but because Jesus taught us not to follow the world but to follow God's love.

Another area in our lives that we should examine to see if we are living a life of Jesus' love is in our writing. I know you are probably thinking that you aren't a writer. I am not speaking about words that you would write in a book, blog, essay, etc. I am speaking of the type of writing most of us do daily. According to the internet in 2021, the average person sends more than forty texts a day. Also, according to the internet, the average office worker writes and sends forty emails a day. Another stat from the internet is that the average person spends 145 minutes a day on various social media platforms.

We have many opportunities to write every day. How many of our text messages are negative? How many of our text messages are used to speak ill of someone? How many of our personal emails talk smack about someone else? How many of our social media posts aren't uplifting? How many of our likes or shared posts on social media are negative? If I'm honest, I have been guilty of all these things. Our written words are just as important as our spoken words. We need to think about what we are writing to others in the same way that we think about what we say to others. Our written words have that same ability to bring life to someone or to harm them. I honestly believe that the written word can be more harmful than spoken words. This is very true for social media posts. If you write negative things about a person, the person has those written words that they can look at over and over again. We need to be aware of this and take caution before we hit send or post.

The last way we show love that I want to touch on is by showing respect. I know that respect is a touchy subject for different age groups. I grew up in the Midwest, and I was taught at a young age to show people respect. I wasn't taught it because of where I grew up but because of the biblical views of respect. There are over twenty-five different scripture passages that are about respecting others, your parents, elders, leaders, and many others. Jesus taught us about respecting others when he taught us to do to others as we would have them do to us (Matt. 7:12). Paul wrote about respecting those in authority (Rom. 13:1-7), respecting others (Coloss. 3:25), and respecting your parents (Eph. 6:1-3). The world has taught the young generations that you only give respect once you have been given respect. Jesus taught the opposite of that. We need to follow Jesus' example and show everyone we come into contact with respect.

- SEVEN -

What Would the World Look Like If We Practiced Christ's Love?

I am not someone who views the world as if it's full of puppies and rainbows. But I do believe that if we were to practice more of Jesus' love, then we would see more of the greater good than the bad. When I talk about puppies and rainbows, I am speaking of only seeing good things in the world. Or that I just see the goodness of God in the world and don't see any of the sins in the world. I know that this world is a fallen place and that ever since the fall of man (to sin) that the world has been changing for the worse. But around 2000 years ago, there was an event that changed the course of the world. That event was the death of Jesus on the cross. Since Jesus died on the cross and was resurrected three days later, the fate of the people of the world has changed. The world is still under the dominion of Satan, but we the people now have a way out of Satan's destiny. His course has already been plotted, and it can't be changed. He committed the one sin that was not forgivable. He said that God is not who he is. But we are blessed to have a way to God, and that is His grace. Grace has a name, and it is Jesus.

If we practiced Jesus' love, there would be a lot more "little Christs" roaming this earth. If we practiced Jesus' love more, then people wouldn't turn away from God because of the way some of His believers acted. The way we treat people can determine whether they believe in Jesus or not. Here are a couple of questions I would like you to think about and answer for yourself. What kind of an aroma are these two different people putting off? Person A is a well-dressed man with a cross around his neck. He is sitting around a table and every fourth word that comes out of his mouth is a swear word. Person B is a man wearing a Christian bikers t-shirt with the sleeves cut off, and his tattoos are showing. Every word that comes out of his mouth is positive and pleasing to the ear. Which person is giving off the aroma of Christ? Which person is giving off the world's aroma? I'm not trying to stereotype or judge people. That is not the point of this example. The point I'm trying to make is that our actions, words, and deeds speak loudly.

In Romans 6: 1-14 (ESV), it says:

> What shall we say then? Are we to continue in sin that grace may abound? By no means! How can we who died to sin still live in it? Do you not know that all of us who have been baptized into Christ Jesus were baptized into his death? We were buried therefore with him by baptism into death, so that, just as Christ was raised from the dead by the glory of the Father, we too might walk in the newness of life. For we have been united with him in a death like his, we shall certainly

be united with him in a resurrection like his. We know that our old self was crucified with him so that the body of sin might be brought to nothing so that we would no longer be enslaved to sin. For one who has died has been set free from sin. Now if we have died with Christ, we believe that we will also live with him. We know that Christ being raised from the dead will never die again; death no longer has dominion over him. For the death he died, he died to sin, once for all, but the life he lives, he lives to God. So, you also must consider yourselves dead to sin and alive to God in Christ Jesus. Let not sin therefore reign in your mortal body to make you obey its passions. Do not present your members to sin as instruments for unrighteousness but present yourselves to God as those who have been brought from death to life and your members to God as instruments for righteousness. For sin will have no dominion over you since you are not under law but under grace.

If we are supposedly representing Jesus, then we should make sure that everything we are doing represents Jesus. The way we talk should represent Jesus. The way we dress should represent Jesus. The way we hold ourselves should represent Jesus. I'm not saying that a Christian has to dress a certain way. I'm not saying a Christian has to have a certain haircut. What I am saying is that Christians should be mindful of how they are representing God and Jesus.

When I was a kid growing up in the Midwest and the weather was hot and humid, I would run around with my shirt off all the time. As a kid, I didn't know what modesty was. After I was an adult and I studied the Word of God more, I was more convicted of how I showed off my body. I realized that my body was the temple of the Lord and that it is meant to be for God (as a temple) and my wife. I became more aware when I would go outside and do yard work or go to the pool or lake and I wasn't wearing a shirt. I wasn't self-conscious of how my body looked (I was a string bean). It was the convictions of the Holy Spirit reminding me to be modest. So fast forward 10-15 years, and I no longer do yardwork without a shirt on. I don't go to the pool without a tank top or shirt on. I believe that the more the Holy Spirit made me aware of how modesty looked for the opposite sex, He also made me aware that modesty is a two-way street. That God wants our bodies to only be seen by our spouses.

The way we talk is another big thing when it comes to representing God. I can remember my first job. I worked at the fastfood restaurant, Hardees, when I turned 16. I remember during the training for that job, there was a section on the language we could and could not use on the job. That was because we weren't just representing ourselves when we were in the restaurant (and in that uniform) we were representing the Hardees company. I can remember the second job I had, also fast food and their training manual. Once again, it was brought up about what language we could and could not use on the job. Even when I spent a little time working retail at Target, there was a section in the training manual about being conscious about the words we use while on the clock. Even in the professional jobs that I have had since college, there has always been a section about appropriate language at every job's training. It's because those companies were telling me that I represented them, and they wanted their image to be held high. So, being a Christian is a kind of uniform for our relationship with God. God wants us to represent him in the best possible way.

James 3:9-12 (NIV) talks about the way we talk. It says:

> With the tongue we praise our Lord and Father, and with it we curse human beings who have been made in God's likeness. Out of the same mouth come praise and cursing. My brothers and sisters, this should not be. Can both fresh water and saltwater flow from the same spring? My brothers and sisters, can a fig tree bear olive or a grapevine bear fig? Neither can a salt spring produce fresh water.

I learned at a young age that there are words that we can say and words that we shouldn't say. I learned at a young age that we shouldn't say mean things to others or about others. I learned a little later in life that some of those words we shouldn't say can be harmful to others. The words we speak can bring blessings to people or they can bring harm to them. It wasn't until a few years ago that I started to fully understand the power of my words.

Also, I have learned how the words I speak to my kids will bring either joy or sorrow to their faces. I learned that if I used a harsh tone or harsh words, it would make my kids sad. I realized that I didn't like being spoken to that way when I was a kid and that made a lightbulb turn on in my head. If I need to correct my kids for something they have done wrong, I will pause and think about how to word what I need to say instead of blurting out whatever is on my tongue. What would it look like if we practiced this in our daily life with every person we interact with? What if when we have an intense conversation with our co-worker about something that went wrong at work and we paused before speaking and thought about how to spin this into a positive mistake that we both can learn from? I'm pretty sure the conversation would be shorter and neither person would regret what was said. What if when we came home from work and we see our spouse for the first time that afternoon, shouldn't we greet them with a smile and some positive words or uplifting words? I'm pretty sure the evening would go smoother than it would if we came in the door and unloaded all our work-related stress on them.

The way we speak and the words we speak are two different actions of the tongue. If we are speaking an ugly four-letter word every other word in a sentence, then we aren't representing God very well. We need to be more conscious of what we say. I am not saying we must be perfect or holier than thou. If we are filling our ears and minds with ugly words, then we are going to start letting ugly words spill from our mouths. You might be thinking in your mind, "What if that is all I hear in the environment I live in or in the environment I work in? That is how the people I hang out with speak, so those words just come out of my mouth." I want to let you know that just like the ugly words coming in your ears can often produce ugly words out of your mouth, so in the same way, peaceful and uplifting words in the ears produce peaceful, and uplifting words coming out of the mouth.

You need to fill your ears and mind with the Word of God. I don't want to sound like a broken record, but Jesus' Word is a lamp to our feet. So, if you struggle with anything that would make you not be a good example of Jesus, please have hope. We don't have to be perfect, but we do need to work on getting closer to Jesus. God loves us even when we are a hot mess; he doesn't need us to clean up before coming to him. Second Corinthians 10: 3-5 (NIV) says:

> For though we live in the world, we do not wage war as the world does. The weapons we fight with are not the weapons of the world. On the contrary, they have divine power to demolish strongholds. We demolish arguments and every pretension that sets itself up against the knowledge of God, and we take captive every thought to make it obedient to Christ.

We may live in this world but the way we live should not be the same as those people that believe in the world's ruler. So, if this world is telling us to dress the way they dress, should we? If the world tells us that we should use the same ugly words it uses, should we? If the world tells us to view each other as objects, should we? If the world tells us to put ourselves above others, should we? The answer to all those questions is the same, and it is no. Sadly, many of us will say no, but still have our big toe dipped in the pool of the world. Some of us hurt our image of being a Christian by the way we dress. I'm not saying that we should wear loose baggy clothes from the top of our heads down to our feet and sing old hymns. We should think about what our dress is making others think about Christ whom we represent.

How confusing is it to see a Christian walking around in the streets wearing a death rock T-shirt when he also has a cross around his neck? Those two articles of clothing contradict each other. This also goes for women who wear very low-cut clothing and a cross necklace. We are trying to bring parts of the world into the Christian life. Proverbs 31:25 (NIV) says, "She is clothed with strength and dignity; she can laugh at the days to come."

I know this might not be a very popular view, but I believe this part of Proverbs 31:25 should pertain to both men and women. We should all be dressed in modesty. Since I believe this, I try to live it out. So, in the summer when it's 85 degrees outside and the sun is blazing down, you will find me mowing the grass in a tank top. Or, if I am at the pool or on a beach, you will see me sitting next to the water with a shirt on. You will even find me in the water with a shirt on. This is me trying to be modest. I believe that God intends for my body to only be seen by my wife.

There have been times while having conversations with other believers that they will get worked up, and the words that come out of their mouths are like that of a sailor. Vulgar words, curse words, negative words, manipulative words, or condescending words—none of these things should be coming out of the mouths of Christians. Using words like that will make non-believers think that those who are Christians are no different from them, which is a valid statement. We are called to be transformed and not to conform to the ways of the world (Rom. 12:2 NIV).

I was listening to a portion of a podcast between a member of a Christian band and their podcast host the other day. I don't know who the host was, or his life story, but some of the words he was saying were saddening to me. The host was interviewing the musician and asked different questions about his life. A question came up about the band's choice to be labeled as a Christian band. The band will play in both Christian and secular venues. The musician's stance was that the band wants to reach people wherever they are, but it can be tricky sometimes when you are labeled a Christian band. And then the host said some words that saddened me. He said that he sometimes doesn't even want to tell others that he is a Christian because of the stigma or reputation that Christians have. I was shocked to hear that, and my first reaction was not great. My first thoughts were a little judgmental (which of course, they shouldn't have been). But after thinking about what he said, I began to be sad. First and foremost, we should never be ashamed of being a Christian. Second, we should never be worried about the stigma or reputation of Christians. If there is a stigma or a reputation of what Christians are, and it's a negative one, then we should be the ones trying to change it.

If we practice Christ's love, then churches would truly have open doors to every person. Let's be very honest here, not all churches are truly open to every person. I have been to churches where it felt warmer outside on a cold day in January in Minnesota than it did in the church (and I'm not talking about the temperature of the building). I have also been to churches where the people were a little too friendly (in my opinion), and it made me want to run out of the building but maybe that was my inner introvert reacting. Years back, I was approached by the youth pastor of the church I was attending to help him make a point during his sermon. He asked me to wear dirty, ratty clothes to church. He wanted me to change my hairstyle and keep my head down so that no one would recognize me. He then observed and had others observe how I was being treated by my fellow members of the church. In his sermon, he made the point that we needed to not look at the outside appearance of people, but we needed to accept everyone.

I think that rings true for the church today. There are many churches that people don't feel comfortable going to because they don't think they will be accepted. Churches (the buildings) should be a hospital for hurting souls. And the Church (the people, the Christians) should be the doctors and nurses for those souls. Jesus healed people's pain while he was on this earth. We, as His church, should be doing the same. People flocked to Jesus because of the truth he told them. People should be flocking to churches because of the truth it speaks about Jesus. People believed that if they just touched Jesus' garments that they would be healed. People should believe that the Church can still receive and give out miracles. The church isn't just for the people who are perfect and healthy. Jesus told us that those people don't exist, and if they act like that, then they are just fooling themselves. Jesus was the only perfect person to walk the earth.

What if the church opened its doors to anyone who wanted to walk in? What if the church didn't have any condemnation or judgment on anyone that walked in? What if we didn't preemptively judge the book by the cover? What if we viewed every person that we see as the soul that they are and not the presumed sinner we think that they are? How much more honest would people be about their struggles? How many more people would be running to the church for healing? The Church should be a place of healing for everyone that enters its building. I can't even count the number of times that I have been struggling with issues, and after being in the presence of Jesus in the church, those issues seemed to shrink. The issues and problems may have still been there, but the fear, worry, and anxiety seemed to disappear. There is something about a compassionate and praying group of people that just makes our burdens disappear. If the body of Christ would act as Jesus showed us to act, then there would be many more people coming to God for help.

Let's be honest, every one of us has needed help from God at some point in our lives. If not, then you are not being honest with yourself. Since God helped you, why wouldn't he want to help everyone else? God looks at sin as sin. He doesn't look at my sin and say it's worse than yours. He saw the disobedience of people and was saddened, but thankfully, Jesus told God that he wanted to be our bridge to God. Church, we need to open our eyes and our hearts. There are real people out there that are hurting. They are doing the best that they can. They are doing what they know to do to take away the pain they are in. Why are we not opening our arms to them? Why are we not going to them and sharing what took us away from the same bondage that has them? I want to challenge each and every person that is reading these words. There are things in your life that you needed Jesus' help with, and he helped you, so please go help others. I have heard from many people that the people that God lays on your heart are the people that are struggling with the same things that Jesus helped you get out of. Go be an example of Jesus to others. The Holy Spirit will lead you to whoever needs your help.

If we practiced Jesus' love for others, then there would be less hate in this world. Hate wouldn't go away, but there would be less. In Matthew 6:24, Jesus is talking to the people about money when He says, "No one can serve two masters. Either you will hate the one and love the other, or you will be devoted to the one and despise the other. You cannot serve both God and money." I know this passage of scripture is talking about putting God above money, but I believe it could also be viewed in another way. If you exchange the word world for the word money, you can see God is wanting us to choose him over this world. Money is a worldly thing so when I read this passage using the word world instead of money, I know we can't serve the two spiritual masters, God, and the fallen angel, Lucifer. Lucifer isn't a Master, but he does have control over the earth at the present time. We can't serve both God who is love, and we can't serve Lucifer, who hates God.

If God is love, and we have committed to follow God, then we can't let that emotion that Lucifer is master over, have control over our lives. I have seen too many people that proclaim Christ with their mouths and give a heart of coal to others that are not the same as them. Simply put, we can't love God and speak hatred toward our fellow man. Jesus said that anyone angry with a brother or sister will be subject to judgment. He compares being angry or hateful towards a fellow person to murdering a fellow person. He said that you will have the same type of judgment from the Father for both of those acts. You can find this in Matthew 5:21-22. We cannot Love God and hate our fellow humans yet that is what some of us do every day. We may not even know that we are doing it. We judge people in our hearts when we see them doing things that we know aren't right. We judge people in our hearts when we see them dressed in a way we find inappropriate. There are some Christians who will outwardly speak hurtful and hateful words to others. When this happens, it's not hard to believe why people don't want to come to church or why people don't want to come to God.

Let's stop condemning others. Let's stop speaking hurtful and hateful things to others. We may not agree with someone's choices, but that does not give us any right to harm them. And we are harming them when we judge with condemnation or use hurtful words or looks. When we do that, all we are doing is throwing more bricks on the path in front of them. And the path that we are paving for them is not leading them to God. The more we do things that give Christians a bad name, the more we are turning people from God and towards Hell. That is not something I want on my shoulders. That is why I purposely and consciously do not judge or say harmful things to people. I do not want to be the reason that someone goes to Hell instead of Heaven. And if I am the reason that someone didn't accept Jesus as their Lord and Savior, then there will be judgment for me when I get to Heaven (See 1 Peter:4 on the topic of suffering for Christ's sake).

So, what are we supposed to do then when we feel that spirit of condemnation come upon us? Get down on your knees and pray for that spirit to leave us. Second, pray for that person. Smile at them. Give them a friendly hello. Do anything but throw judgment and hatred toward them. When I have had the spirit of condemnation come upon myself, I have done just what I said. I prayed for that spirit to leave me, and then I prayed for that person. They may never know that I prayed for them, but I did, and if there was eye contact, I smiled and said something nice to them. I'll leave you with some of Jesus' most famous words on judging others. Matthew 7:1-5 (NIV) says:

> Do not judge, or you too will be judged. For in the same way, you judge others, you will be judged, and with the measure you use, it will be measured to you. Why do you look at the speck of sawdust in your brother's eye and pay no attention to the plank in your own eye? How can you say to your brother, 'Let me take the speck out of your eye,' when all the time there is a plank in your own eye? You hypocrite, first take the plank out of your own eye, and then you will see clearly to remove the speck from your brother's eye.'

Let us first remove the plank out of our eye so we can see clearly how God wants us to help our brother get the speck from their eye.

Lastly, if we acted more like Jesus, then there would be more persecution of Christians. Jesus was attacked for most of His ministry. There were many times that Jesus told His disciples that because they followed him, they would be persecuted. The more of Jesus' love that we spread and share with others, the angrier Satan gets. He does not want us excelling and bringing more people to God, so Satan will use (and is using) the things of this world to try to persuade Christians against showing God's love. Have you ever noticed that the more that you are in God's will for your life, the more Satan attacks you? I have noticed that more and more as I write this book. I am writing this book because the Holy Spirit led me to write it. Ever since I started to write it, Satan has been attacking me. It hasn't been a physical attack, but more of an attack in my mind. He likes to remind me of who I was and what I have done. I'm not perfect, but I am doing the perfect will of God. The more we are showing God's love to others, the more Satan will counterattack. The more we make the church more like a hospital, the more Satan will try to attack the Church. We are already seeing that now. I am friends with some pastors that had their churches morally attacked. The pastors are doing God's will, the church is growing, and miracles are happening at their church. But they are being attacked by people in the community that don't want a Bible-believing, Holy Spirit-lead church. They stood their ground, and the church has done nothing but grow more. We should not be surprised by the attacks on God's church since Jesus was attacked. We need to stand firm on the word of the Lord. God will always be with us as long as we are with him and are putting him first.

Let's be the hands and feet of Jesus. Be the hands and feet of Jesus in your community, in your family, in your school, and at your workplace. The more we are loving others as Jesus loved us, the more His Spirit will be working in others.

- EIGHT -

Let's Apply How to Live Out Christ's Love

As I sit here writing these words to you, I am not writing words I think are wise, or that are grand. I am writing words that I hope will encourage you. Words to lift you up. Words that will move you to dig deeper into your relationship with Jesus. Words that will reflect how much Jesus loves you and shows you how he wants you to love others. We all know that this world is just a temporary place for us. These bodies of ours are fleeting, and this world will not last forever. So, if we call ourselves Christians then we should live like the One we are representing.

For us to make a difference in this world we first need to Love God. If you are reading this book, and you feel that you don't truly have a close relationship with God then please read through the Gospels (Matthew, Mark, Luke, and John) to get to know who Jesus is. Once you realize what he did for you, you will not be the same. You will not want to live the same life that you are currently living, or were living. If this, is you, please visit a local church that is a Bible-believing church and one that is on fire for God. There are many resources online to learn more about God. If you have realized that you don't have a personal relationship with Jesus and you want a relationship and not just religion. You just need to have faith in Jesus, in who the Bible says he is. You need to ask Jesus to come into your life and have a relationship with him. All it takes is a simple little prayer to Jesus asking him to come into your life and have a relationship with you. Asking him to forgive you for all of your wrongdoings against him and others.

Second, we also need to start living our lives for God. I'm sure you have heard this said many times, but it is true. There is nothing wrong with working hard to create a good life for you, and your family, but as Christians, we are called to do more than just look out for ourselves. As Christians, we are called to share the good news of what Jesus did in our lives with those around us. God the Father sent His son Jesus to be an example for us, and a savior for us. Jesus told us that he had to go back to the Father so that the Holy Spirit could come, and be our helper. To live a life for God, we need to allow the Holy Spirit to be our helper. He will help us know what we should do. He will help us when we are struggling with the stuff that the enemy Satan is throwing at us. He will help guide us to those that are in need. He will guide us on how to help others. He will even show us what to do to bring praise to God. The more, and more we live for God the more, and more God's love will spill out of us like a bottlecap under a faucet of running water. We need to be living our lives for God's will, and not for our own will.

When we are living in God's will then we have a much better chance of positively affecting someone else's life. We will have the desire to help others who may or may not know God. Anyone can help someone else, but how much greater is the impact going to be if the person doing the help is a Christ follower? The impact could be an eternal one. Christ's followers are helping with a purpose, with a desire to help the other person skip Hell and head towards Heaven. Isn't that what we are all called to do anyways? Jesus' last commission to His disciples before heading back up to heaven was to "Go and make disciples of all nations, baptizing them in the name of the Father, and of the Son, and of the Holy Spirit, and teaching them to obey everything I have commanded you" (Matt. 28:18-20 NIV).

There might be some who will say that God won't want them. That they have done too many wrong things. Guess what? We all have done wrong things, and God knows that, and he is gracious, and forgives us. He forgives us of our sins, and then he forgets them when we have a relationship with Jesus. God is a merciful Father. Once we ask God for forgiveness through the blood of His son Jesus, all of those wrong things are erased from our records. It's just like when you are typing something using an old-school typewriter, and you misspell a word. Jesus' blood is like the whiteout a writer uses to cover up their mistake. The sin is only known to the one who did it, just like the misspelled word is only visible to the one who wrote it. God chooses to forgive our sins, and then he chooses to forget them. There is only one sin that God will not forgive, and that sin is denying who he is and denying who Jesus is.

When we are living our life for God, and we are tapped into the Holy Spirit as our friend, and helper then we will have no option but to love God the way he asked us to love him. If we are loving God the way that he asked us to love Him, then we are living to be loving to others the way that he has asked us to love them. It is a ripple effect like when you throw a rock into a pond where the water is perfectly still. Or just like the water in the bottlecap example, I used earlier. The more and more we love God, he is the faucet, His love is the water, and we are the bottlecap. The love that he pours into us will continue to spill out of us and onto those around us. I don't know about you, but I truly want His love to spill on those around me. If we stumble, then we just have to bring that stumbling block back before God, and then get right back to His will.

If you don't know how to start loving others, here are a couple of verses that we can read, and then we can take action. The first one is to love your enemy. In Luke 6:27-36 (NIV), it says:

> But to you who are listening I say: Love your ene-mies, do good to those who hate you, bless those who curse you, pray for those who mistreat you. If someone slaps you on one cheek, turn to them the other also. If someone takes your coat, do not with-hold your shirt from them. Give to everyone who asks you, and if anyone takes what belongs to you, do not demand it back. Do to others as you would have them do to you. If you love those who love you, what credit is that to you? Even sinners love those who love them. And if you do good to those who are good to you, what credit is that to you? Even sinners do that. And if you lend to those from whom you expect repay-ment, what credit is that to you? Even sinners lend to

sinners, expecting to be repaid in full. But love your enemies, do good to them, and lend to them without expecting to get anything back. Then your reward will be great, and you will be children of the Most High because he is kind to the ungrateful and wicked. Be merciful, just as your father is merciful.

Guess what? Once we sin (and we all do) we become an enemy of God. We have chosen to go against what God asked of us. But by grace and Jesus' blood, God showed us, love. He loved us even though we mistreated Him. He loved us even when we slapped him across the face. He loved us even when we took His coat and shirt. God loved us when we took what was His, and we didn't give it back. That love He still gave us was His son Jesus. He also gave us grace for when we make mistakes again and again. Grace is another big bottle of whiteout.

Another verse is one we discussed earlier. Do not judge others, the world does enough of that for all of us. For Matthew 7:1-5 (NIV) says:

Do not judge, or you too will be judged. For in the same way, you judge others, you will be judged, and with the measure you use, it will be measured to you. Why do you look at the speck of sawdust in your brother's eye and pay no attention to the plank in your own eye? How can you say to your brother, 'Let me take the speck out of your eye,' when all the

time there is a plank in your own eye? You hypocrite,
first take the plank out of your own eye, and then
you will see clearly to remove the speck from your
brother's eye.

There is too much judgment coming from people in this world.
God did not command us to judge others. He said we should not
judge others. If we do judge others, then we will be judged by God
in the same way. I don't know about you, but I don't like being
judged, and I don't want to give God any more things to judge me
about. God will give us grace when we are judged for the sins that
put Jesus on the cross, so we should show others grace too and not
be judgmental of them. Do we make Jesus irresistible to people or
do we make Jesus repulsive to people? Think about that next time
you are about to judge someone who is doing something that you
don't agree with. Our whole purpose should be to bring Jesus to
everyone. That was the last thing Jesus commanded us to do.

Another important passage about love is 1 Corinthians 13,
which is typically viewed by most people as the love chapter in the
New Testament. You hear verses 4 through 8 at a lot of weddings.
These verses show us what love is like. It shows us the traits of unconditional love. I would like to go through verses 1-3 first.

If I speak in the tongues of men or of Angels, but do not
have unconditional love, I am only a resounding gong
or a clanging cymbal. If I have the gift of prophecy
and can fathom all mysteries and all knowledge, and

if I have a faith that can move mountains, but do not
have unconditional love, I am nothing. If I give all I
have to the poor and give over my body to hardship
that I may boast, but do not have unconditional love,
I gain nothing.

While meditating on these verses, I had a thought come into
my spirit. I have been talking a lot about how Jesus is our example
of love and how he was love for us. He is an example of how we are
to love others, and God gave Him to us to be His symbol of love
to us. The thought that came to my spirit was, what if we exchange
Jesus for the word love? These verses are talking about if we do these
different types of actions or work but don't have love, then they
are meaningless. Think about it as if we do all these kind actions
to people, but we are just going through the motions, then it is all
for nothing. Our hearts and our soul are not backing those actions.
Actions without heart are just nice motions, but not much else.

When we have Christ in our lives, then everything we do
should be with heart. There should be meaning behind every
action. Everything we do should be things that honor God. Our
symbols (actions) of love should be shown with heart. I know I
have been guilty of just being a clanging cymbal. I have shown love
but it was just a motion or action. There have been times that I have
seen someone who was needing help getting something at a store.
My heart and mind weren't focused on Christ at that time, and my
actions showed it. I was nice to the person and helped reach the
item they needed, but I wasn't being cheerful, I wasn't smiling and

I'm sure my attitude was showing that I thought it was an inconvenience to help that person. That was a kind act, but it wasn't an act of love. I want to speak in the tongues of men and have love. I want the person that I am talking to, to see Christ in the words I use. And it's not just the actual words, but the tone and the attitude in my voice. If any of that is off, then I am just being a resounding gong. So, in 1 Corinthians 13:1-8 (replacing Jesus for Love) it would say:

> If I speak in the tongues of men, or of Angels, but do not have Jesus, I am only a resounding gong or a clanging cymbal. If I have the gift of prophecy and can fathom all mysteries and all knowledge, and if I have a faith that can move mountains, but do not have Jesus, I am nothing. If I give all I have to the poor and give over my body to hardship that I may boast, but do not have Jesus, I gain nothing. Jesus is patient, Jesus is kind. He does not envy, He does not boast, He is not proud. He does not dishonor others, He is not self-seeking, He is not easily angered, and He keeps no record of wrongs. Jesus does not delight in evil but rejoices with the truth. Jesus always protects, always trust, always hopes, always perseveres. Jesus never fails.

There are great benefits when you love the way Jesus loved us. We will reap in heaven what we sow here on earth. I know I reap a ton of joy when I sow Jesus' love into other people. When I listen to the Holy Spirit and follow His direction, I immediately reap what

I've sown into others in the way of joy and peace. Another benefit we get from loving others as Jesus intended is that we will love to be alive. The reason we love to live is simply that we are living to love others. When you love like Jesus, you will live your best life. Are you loving to live? Are you living to Love?

Third, a benefit I believe we get by loving others the way Jesus loved is that the more love we spread, the more that love will heal our pain. I have seen evidence of this in my own life. In my twenties, I was going through a tough valley in my life, but I continued to be in God's love and to give out His love to others. I was helping in the kids' ministries, Awana, and in Upward Basketball. I was showing God's love to those kids, and in the process, God was healing the wounds I had from that tough valley. Another example of God healing my pain is through another ministry that I have had the privilege to be involved in. I have had the privilege to go into prisons and bring the Gospel of Jesus to the inmates there. I had no idea how much healing I would get by going inside the prison walls and loving on the inmates. The wound that it healed was my grandparent's death. My grandparents were murdered when I was a young child. I had suppressed those feelings of loss for a long time, but when I was asked to help with the prison ministry, those memories, and feelings came flooding back. I'm sure it was Satan trying to do whatever he could to limit my effect on the inmates. Bringing those memories and feelings out meant that I had to deal with them, and God amazingly dealt with them.

My wife and I have now gone into five different prisons over the years to minister to the inmates. Some of the prisons were for men and some were for women. When we do these ministries, we get the privilege of bringing a talk about a predetermined topic about God to the inmates. Two of those five times, I had the privilege to talk about God's love to them. I will say that talking about God's love is one of my favorite things to talk about when speaking about God. The last time we were at a women's prison, my wife and I had the privilege to give a talk about God's love. She talked to the women about her story and God as a Father figure, and then I gave my talk. Well, as it goes with a lot of things, the Holy Spirit decided that someone in the room needed to hear something different about God's love than what I had planned so I spoke about one of my favorite passages that deal with love.

I started by talking about scripture that I think is very relevant to loving others as Jesus wants us to love them which can be found in Revelations 3:15-16 (NIV). This is where Jesus is talking to one of the seven churches in the book of Revelations, the group of people gathering in His name, and not the building. He says, "I know your deeds, that you are neither cold nor hot. I wish you were either one or the other! So, because you are lukewarm – neither hot nor cold – I am about to spit you out of my mouth." The relevance of those verses is that Jesus is calling out a group of believers for not being on fire for him, or not just ignoring him. The church was lukewarm or wishy-washy. They were a group of believers who were so well off that they didn't think they needed anything from God. They remembered that God blessed them, but they weren't thankful or good stewards of those blessings. Jesus doesn't want us to be lukewarm or wishy-washy. Jesus doesn't want us to get saved and then say, "Well, my soul is safe, so I am going to continue to live life the way I want to." I think too many believers live their lives like this. Too many people are just checking the box to save themselves, but they don't want to grow up and change.

When Paul talked to the church in Corinth, he talks about what it is like when we first get saved. We are like an infant, and we have to only drink milk, but just like a child, we can't survive on just milk. We need to get protein and vegetables. We need to mature in our faith. We can't mature if we are living a life for ourselves. Living a life of selfish desires sounds like a life of an infant. If you are a 30, 40, or 50-year-old "infant in Christ" when you meet Jesus in person, he might quote Revelations 3:15 to you. Your storehouse in heaven might just be bare. I plead with you to not be lukewarm in your relationship with Jesus. I plead that you won't be cold either. Please, for your sake, and the sake of the people of this broken world, let's be hot for Jesus.

After speaking to the ladies at the prison about Revelations 3:15-16, I told them the story about Jesus' meeting with the disciples after he was resurrected and returned to the earth. Jesus' conversation with Peter is found in John 21:15-19. As a youth, I heard a message about this scripture, and I never looked at the passage the same. After Jesus and the disciples had finished eating, Jesus straight-up called Peter out (Peter had denied that he knew Jesus three times the night that Jesus was betrayed and given over to the Roman soldiers). And it wasn't in a good way, either. Jesus said to Peter, "Simon, son of John, do you love me more than these?" If you review this passage using the original Greek then you will see that in the Greek language, there are multiple different words used for love. The Greek Bible typically used four different words for love, and each one of those words is a different type of love. The four most common words were eros – intimate love, storge – family love (mother, father, brother or sister), philia – friendship or brotherly love (Philadelphia is the city of brotherly love), and agape – unconditional love (God's love for us).

So, if we mix the text with English words and the Greek word for love, it would read like the following: "Simon, son of John, do you Agape me more than these?" Peter answered Jesus saying, "Yes, Lord, you know that I philia you." Jesus answered back, "Feed my lambs." Then Jesus asked him a second time, "Simon, son of John, do you agape me?" Peter answered saying "Yes, Lord, you know that I philia you." Jesus replied, "Tend my sheep." Then Jesus asked a third time, "Simon, son of John, do you philia me?" At this, Peter was grieved because Jesus said to him a third time, "Do you philia me?" Peter said to Jesus, "Lord, you know everything. You know that I philia you." Jesus said to him, "Feed my sheep. Very truly I tell you, when you were younger, you dressed yourself and went where you wanted but when you are old, you will stretch out your hand, and someone else will dress you and lead you where you do not want to go." Jesus said this to indicate the kind of death by which Peter would glorify God. Then Jesus said to him, "Follow me!" (John 21:15-19).

Whenever I read this passage in the Word, I always react to it as if I were in Peter's shoes. How would I respond to Jesus if he asked me if I Agape him? I'm sure verbally I would say, "Sure, I Agape you" but deep down in my heart and soul, is that the true answer? If I do truly love Jesus unconditionally then there should be no limit to how I will prove to him that I love him. If he asked me to pack up my family and move across the country to meet someone who needs to know Jesus, would I? What if he asked me to leave my family to go minister to a tribe of people in Africa, would I? Do we love Jesus with true Agape love? Jesus has never asked me to pack up my family and move. He hasn't asked me to move to Africa but He has asked me to love my neighbors. He has asked me to love my enemies. He has asked me to forgive others that have deeply hurt me. He has asked me to give money to people I don't know. He has asked me to give my time to help those who need help.

We live in a time where having a deep-rooted faith in Jesus isn't going to cost us our lives as it did Peter who died as an old man and was hung on a cross. Jesus' words were fulfilled by the type of death that Peter had. Even though we don't live in a culture that requires us to die for our faith in Jesus, we do live in a culture that doesn't want us to be vocal about our relationship with Jesus. It's okay for us to drive around with a bumper sticker on our car that is in the shape of a fish, but it's not okay to share our opinion if it's different from the world. It's okay to post a meme on social media that is a Bible verse, but it's not okay to comment on someone's picture of them drunk if your opinion isn't the same as theirs. It's okay to walk around wearing a t-shirt that says, "Jesus is my homeboy," but it's not okay to question someone's faith in God. How will I respond when Jesus says, "My son/daughter, do you Agape me? Then tell the truth about me." Then ask that Christian posting inappropriate things on

Facebook about their maturity in me." "My son/daughter, do you Agape me? Then go tell the world about me. Even if that means the world will expose that you are not perfect. Even if that means the world will try to drag your name into the dirt. Even if that means every person you know turns their back on you. Do you Agape me?

I'm not saying any of those things will happen, but what if they did? How will we respond to Jesus? Will we stand firm in His Word that says He will never leave us or forsake us? Will we simply say to Jesus, I philia you, but I can't go and do those things? Maybe Jesus has already asked you the same question, and you answered that is too hard. If you are still on this earth and you are still breathing, then your time is not up. You have every chance to turn back to Jesus and start loving him as He loves us. Honestly, I have been Peter more times in my life than I want to admit. I have told Jesus that he is wrong, and that I'm not the right man for the job. I was Peter for a couple of years when it came to this book. I would dismiss the Holy Spirit tugging on my heart when it came to writing. I even went as far as have a conversation with God Himself. I told him that I am not a writer. I am not good at speaking words to people. I use simple words when I speak because I don't want to embarrass myself. But the Holy Spirit continued to give me gentle nudges. I finally agreed to the Holy Spirit's request to write, and I started to write a story. But that is not what God wanted me to write. He said to write about love. About how He loves us and how we are to love others. Once again, I tried to get God to compromise on the request. Guess who won that battle? It was God, and I hope that by my obedience to God's calling, someone out there will then in return listen to God's direction in their life. Listen to the Holy Spirit, and follow His direction.

If we are in God's Word every day and have our souls' ears open to the Holy Spirit, then we will be ready to do the things God wants us to do for others. Doing the things of God for others is the love that we are showing. Let's show this world that Christian is not just a word and that being a Christian is someone who loves others unconditionally. You might run into someone who has heard of Jesus but doesn't believe in Him, and you are the example of Jesus to them. God is asking that we love like Jesus, and judge just like Jesus judged the adulteress at the well. He asked her for water instead of condemning her for her past. He even went as far as telling her that he was able to get her water that would never cause her to thirst. He was trying to explain to her that he is that living water. We can share that same water with others also.

Jesus is love. Let's make love our priority. Do you make Jesus irresistible to people, or do you make Jesus repulsive to people? When you love God more than yourself, then the closer you will get to him. The closer you get to God, you can do nothing but mature in your relationship with God. The more you mature in your relationship with God, the more you will be used by God. The more you are used by God, the more you can be God's unconditional love to the world. Let's be God's unconditional love. Let's make a difference and be God's love to others.

Scripture references for God's Love To Us

Loving your enemies

Luke 6:27-36 (NIV): But to you who are listening I say: Love your enemies, do good to those who hate you, bless those who curse you, pray for those who mistreat you. If someone slaps you on one cheek, turn to them the other also. If someone takes your coat, do not withhold your shirt from them. Give to everyone who asks you, and if anyone takes what belongs to you, do not demand it back. Do to others as you would have them do to you. If you love those who love you, what credit is that to you? Even sinners love those who love them. And if you do good to those who are good to you, what credit is that to you? Even sinners do that. And if you lend to those from whom you expect repayment, what credit is that to you? Even sinners lend to sinners, expecting to be repaid in full. But love your enemies, do good to them, and lend to them without expecting to get anything back. Then your reward will be great, and you will be children of the Most High because he is kind to the ungrateful and wicked. Be merciful, just as your father is merciful.

Feed my sheep love in action

John 21:15-17: When they had finished eating, Jesus said to Simon Peter, "Simon, son of John, do you love me more than these?" "Yes, Lord," he said, "you know that I love you." Jesus said, "Feed my lambs." Again, Jesus said, "Simon, son of John, do you love me?" He answered, "Yes, Lord, you know that I love you." Jesus said, "Take care of my sheep." The third time he said to him, "Simon, son of John, do you love me?" Peter was hurt because Jesus asked him the third time, "Do you love me?" He said, "Lord, you know all things; you know that I love you." Jesus said, "Feed my sheep."

1 John 3:19 (NIV): Dear children, let us not love with words or speech but with actions and in truth.

John 3:16 (NIV): For God so loved the world that he gave his one and only Son, that whoever believes in him shall not perish but have eternal live.

2 Corinthians 5:21 (NIV): God made him who had no sin to be sin for us, so that in him we might become the righteousness of God.

1 John 3:16-18 (NIV): This is how we know what love is: Jesus Christ laid down his life for us. And we ought to lay down our lives for our brothers and sisters. If anyone has material possessions and sees a brother or sister in need but has no pity on them, how can the love of God be in that person?

Romans 8:32 (NIV): He who did not spare his own Son, but gave him up for us all – how will he not also, along with him, graciously give us all things?

Romans 8:35-39 (NIV): Who shall separate us from the love of Christ? Shall trouble or hardship or persecution or famine or nakedness or danger or sword? As it is written, "For your sake we face death all day long; we are considered as sheep to be slaughtered." No, in all these things we are more than conquerors through him who loved us. For I am convinced that neither death nor life, neither angels nor demons, neither the present nor the future, nor any powers, neither height nor depth, nor anything else in all creation, will be able to separate us from the love of God that is in Christ Jesus our Lord.

Romans 5:8 (NIV): But God demonstrates his own love for us in this: While we were still sinners, Christ died for us.

Ephesians 2:6-10 (NIV): And God raised us up with Christ and seated us with him in the heavenly realms in Christ Jesus, in order that in the coming ages he might show the incomparable riches of his grace, expressed in his kindness to us in Christ Jesus. For it is by grace you have been saved, through faith – and this is not from yourselves, it is the gift of God – not by works, so that no one can boast. For we are God's handiwork, created in Christ Jesus to do good works, with God prepared in advance for us to do.

Jeremiah 31:3 (NIV): The Lord appeared to us in the past, saying, "I have loved you with an everlasting love; I have drawn you with unfailing kindness."

Love one another

John 13:34-35 (NIV): A new command I give you: Love one another. As I have loved you, so you must love one another. By this everyone will know that you are my disciples if you love one another.

1 John 3:11-15 (NIV): For this is the message you heard from the beginning. We should love one another. Do not be like Cain, who belonged to the evil one and murdered his brother. And why did he murder him? Because his own actions were evil, and his brothers were righteous. Do not be surprised, my brothers and sisters, if the world hates you. We know that we have passed from death to life because we love each other. Anyone who does not love remains in death. Anyone who hates a brother or sister is a murderer, and you know that no murderer has eternal life residing in him.

Galatians 5:6 (NIV): For in Christ Jesus, neither circumcision nor uncircumcision has any value. The only thing that counts is faith expressing itself through love.

1 John 5:2-3 (NIV): This is how we know that we love the children of God: by loving God and carrying out his commands. In fact, this is love for God: to keep his commands. And his commands are not burdensome.

1 Corinthians 13:13 (NIV): And now these three remain: faith, hope and love. But the greatest of these is love.

Ephesians 5:1-2 (NIV): Follow God's example, therefore, as dearly loved children and walk in the way of love, just as Christ loved us and gave himself up for us as a fragrant offering and sacrifice to God.

Luke 6:45 (NIV): A good man brings good things out of the good stored up in his heart, and an evil man brings evil things out of the evil stored up in his heart. For the mouth speaks what the heart is full of.

God's power to forgive

Romans 8:1-2 (NIV): Therefore, there is now no condemnation for those who are in Christ Jesus, because through Christ Jesus the law of the Spirit who gives life has set you free from the law of sin and death.

1 John 1:9 (NIV): If we confess our sins, he is faithful and just and will forgive us our sins and purify us from all unrighteousness.

1 John 3:20-21 (NIV): If our hearts condemn us, we know that God is greater than our hearts, and he knows everything. Dear friends, if our hearts do not condemn us, we have confidence before God.

Ephesians 3:16-21 (NIV): I pray that out of his glorious riches he may strengthen you with power through his Spirit in your inner being so that Christ may dwell in your hearts through faith. And I pray that you, being rooted and established in love, may have power, together with all the Lord's holy people, to grasp how wide and long and high and deep is the love of Christ, and to know this love that surpasses knowledge – that you may be filled to the measure of all the fullness of God. Now to him who is able to do immeasurably more than all we ask or imagine, according to his power that is within us, to him be glory in the church and in Christ Jesus throughout all generations, for ever and ever! Amen.

Faith and trust in God

Hebrews 11:6 (NIV): And without faith it is impossible to please God because anyone who comes to him must believe that he exists and that he rewards those who earnestly seek him.

Matthew 6:33 (NIV): But seek first his kingdom and his righteousness, and all these things will be given to you as well.

Romans 2:4 (NIV): Or do you show contempt for the riches of his kindness, forbearance, and patience, not realizing that God's kindness is intended to lead you to repentance?

Matthew 6:19-21 (NIV): Do not store up for yourselves treasures on earth, where moths and vermin destroy, and where thieves break in and steal. But store up for yourselves treasures in heaven, where moths and vermin do not destroy, and where thieves do not break in and steal. For where your treasure is, there your heart will be also.

1 Corinthians 14:1 (NIV): Follow the way of love and eagerly desire gifts of the Spirit, especially prophecy.

Ephesians 3:14-19 (NIV): For this reason, I kneel before the Father, from whom every family in heaven and on earth derives its name. I pray that out of his glorious riches he may strengthen you with power through his Spirit in your inner being, so that Christ may dwell in your hearts through faith. And I pray that you, being rooted and established in love, may have power, together with all the Lord's holy people, to grasp how wide and long and high and deep is the love of Christ, and to know this love that surpasses knowledge, that you may be filled to the measure of all the fullness of God.

God's love calls, confirms, justifies, glorifies, and defends.
Romans 8:28-36 (NIV): And we know that in all things God works for the good of those who love him, who have been called according to his purpose. For those God foreknew he also predestined to be conformed to the image of his Son, that he might be the firstborn among many brothers and sisters. And those he predestined, he also called; those he called, he also justified; those he justified, he also glorified. What, then, shall we say in response to these things? If God is for us, who can be against us? He who did not spare his own Son, but gave him up for us all-how will he not also, along with him, graciously give us all things? Who will bring any charge against those whom God has chosen: It is God who justifies. Who then is the one who condemns? No one. Christ Jesus who died-more than that who was raised to life-is at the right hand of God and is also

interceding for us. Who shall separate us from the love of Christ? Shall trouble or hardship or persecution or famine or nakedness or danger or sword? As it is written:

"For your sake we face death all day long; we are considered as sheep to be slaughtered."

Acknowledgments

J ust like life, writing a book takes you on a journey. This journey would not have happened without the help of my village. I am so blessed to have been surrounded by so many Godly people who were willing to give their time and thoughts to help with this book. First and foremost, I must thank the Holy Spirit for the nudges over the past few years. Without the Holy Spirit's nudges and wisdom, I would never have written this book. I am so thankful to my sister, Beth Foreman, for her critique of this book in its first iteration. I am thankful that you didn't hold anything back just because I am your brother.

I am so thankful that God placed my family under the teaching of Pastor Shaun and Amy Gustafson. One of their sermons pushed me to surrender to the Holy Spirit's call for this book. Thank you to Kim Medin for your edits to this book. Your whole family has been such a blessing to our family.

A lot of this book wouldn't be what it is without the guidance and mentoring I got as a youth. I want to give a big thank you to Eugene Tindall for helping me with my walk with God. You and Anne taught me lessons that I still use to this day. Thank you for teaching me so I can now hopefully pass that knowledge on to others. D Allen Smith for your help with the final touches for the book.

I have to thank my wonderful wife for being patient with me over the last few years. It was your encouragement that helped me to keep pushing when I would struggle to keep the book moving. It was your words of affirmation that helped me believe that I could write this book. It was your knowledge of the Holy Spirit that helped me to trust in the Holy Spirit when he asked me to write this book. Thank you for the final critiques of this book. Your knowledge is vast. I also want to thank my children for being the awesome kids they are and for always pushing me to be more Christ-like for their sake and for the sake of others. I want to thank my parents for raising me in a Christian household. For encouraging me to go to church and learn about God.

I want to thank all those that read this book. It is my prayer that you will let the Holy Spirit work on your heart and that you will let him guide you as you mature in your relationship with Jesus.

9 781662 872334